Reggio Emilia Encounters

The documentation of young children's learning plays a vital role in the preschools of Reggio Emilia. This cutting edge approach to bringing record-keeping and assessment into the heart of young children's learning is envied and emulated by educators around the world.

This inspiring book is based upon a Documentation approach successfully implemented by Stirling Council in Scotland, whose preschool educators experienced dramatic improvements in their understanding of young children, how they learn and the potential unleashed by successfully engaging families in the learning process. This approach, which is based on careful listening to children and observation of their interests and concerns, centres around recording and commentating on children's learning through photos, wall displays, videos and a variety of different media.

This follow-up text is an accessible and lively companion to *An Encounter with Reggio Emilia: Children's Early Learning Made Visible*. It will encourage the reader to develop a deeper understanding of the approach and will show how the authors have seen a complete paradigm shift for those already working with documentation as a result of the guidance laid out in their previous book. Drawing on the experiences of educators and collaborators, the authors offer a framework from which any early years educator can easily adapt and develop in their own educational setting.

Pat Wharton is an early years pedagogical consultant, Stirling, UK.

Linda Kinney was formerly Assistant Chief Executive, Stirling Council, UK.

Reggio Emilia Encounters

Children and adults in collaboration

Edited by
Pat Wharton and Linda Kinney

Routledge
Taylor & Francis Group

LONDON AND NEW YORK

First published 2015
by Routledge
2 Park Square, Milton Park, Abingdon, Oxon OX14 4RN

and by Routledge
711 Third Avenue, New York, NY 10017

Routledge is an imprint of the Taylor & Francis Group, an informa business

British Library Cataloguing in Publication Data
A catalogue record for this book is available from the British Library

Library of Congress Cataloging in Publication Data
Wharton, Pat.
Reggio Emilia encounters : children and adults in collaboration / Pat Wharton and Linda Kinney.
pages cm
1. Reggio Emilia approach (Early childhood education)—Scotland—Stirling (County)
2. Observation (Educational method) I. Kinney, Linda, 1956– II. Title.
LB1029.R35W47 2015
372.2109413'12—dc23
2014029238

ISBN: 978-1-138-84174-1 (hbk)
ISBN: 978-1-138-02314-7 (pbk)
ISBN: 978-1-315-73196-4 (ebk)

Typeset in Galliard
by FiSH Books Ltd, Enfield

Printed and bound by CPI Group (UK) Ltd, Croydon, CR0 4YY

Contents

Foreword

Stirling Council, since its inception in 1996, has believed in the importance of providing, promoting and developing early years provision for children and families. This belief is based on our commitment to ensuring the best possible start for our youngest children and our understanding that good early years provision can benefit children and enhance family wellbeing.

The dedication of our early years professionals and partners has led us to understand more fully that the way in which we see and think about children has a significant impact not only on the types of early years provision we make available, but also the place of children in our society. We have learned about the importance of making early learning visible, thereby making evident the richness, resourcefulness and the amazing capabilities of children. This way of thinking and working with children has been inspiring for those of us involved in supporting and promoting public services for children, families and communities.

Our vision for early years provision in Stirling came about as a result of a political commitment and local drive to develop early years provision in a time when services were patchy and there was no universal entitlement to early learning. Extensive consultation took place with parents, with children and with early years experts locally, nationally and internationally. The outcome was that parents told us they wanted early years services to understand their child as an individual; that above all else they wanted their children to play and learn, make friends and to be happy. Parents also wanted services that were flexible in opening hours to accommodate work patterns and were places that were safe but also stimulating. Children told us that they wanted to be able to play outdoors, to be able to create things and to make friends and learn. Our wide range of experts and our studies of provision in Scandinavia and in Europe told us about the importance of good quality early years provisions and in particular, the key elements that would be of most benefit to children and families. This included well-qualified adults and ongoing professional development, high quality environments with outdoor spaces, an early learning curriculum model and political and strategic leadership.

Our thinking and discussions about the importance of the early years continues today. Our conversations are now being enhanced by developments taking place at national level, including the publication of the Scottish Government's Early Years Framework 2008, the universal entitlement to15 hours per week of early learning for all three- and four-year olds and some two-year olds in Scotland 2014. The establishment of the Early Years Collaborative in 2013 aimed at bringing together Community Planning Partners including education, health, police, voluntary sector and local communities to work together to develop early years services.

However, it is essential that in our discussions we continue to ensure children remain at the centre of our conversations. It was the vision and practice in Reggio Emilia that provided an early inspiration for our team in Stirling and it is the 'hundred languages of children' that continues to influence our early years practice in Stirling today. The building and development of a model of pedagogical documentation in Stirling that reflects our cultural and organisational values is the outcome of this influence. This approach to early learning and our understandings of working in this way is at the core of this book.

I hope that you too can be inspired by the work of the dedicated and committed people that have contributed to this book, not least by the open and honest way in which they too make visible their learning, their vulnerabilities and their strengths as people and as early educators.

Bob Jack
Chief Executive, Stirling Council

List of contributors

Pat Wharton, Early Years Consultant (Early Learning Associates) previously Senior Early Childhood Link Officer, Stirling Council

Liz Greig, Early Years Consultant, formerly Reader in Early Education, Dundee University

Karen McLaughlin, Head of Doune and Wellgreen nurseries, Stirling Council

Yvonne Thomson, Acting Depute, Doune Nursery, Stirling

Sharron McIntosh, Early Years Educator, Park Drive Nursery, Stirling Council

Annie Miller, Retired Head of Croftamie and Doune Nurseries, Stirling Council

Lorna Willow, Head of Croftamie and Doune Nurseries, Stirling Council

Jackie Dupont, Pedagogista, Stirling Council

Wendie Garnett, Pedagogista, Stirling Council

Brian Hartley, Artist, Still Motion, Glasgow

Sharon Milne, Pedagogista, Stirling Council

Tanya Starkey, Principal Teacher, Callander Primary School, Stirling Council

Linda Kinney, recently retired Assistant Chief Executive, Stirling Council, previously Head of Learning and Development, Stirling Council.

Acknowledgements

We would like to thank the children, not only those who appear within the pages of this book, but also those within all the settings across the Stirling Council area who they represent. Thanks also go to the early years educators who have had the courage to contribute to this book and share their experiences with the reader. In their recording of their experiences the voices of their fellow colleagues both in Stirling and Angus are also heard and represented. We would also like to congratulate them on the honest way in which they have described their encounters with Reggio Emilia and their intention to continue to be inspired by its impact on the children and families with whom they collaborate.

Appreciation must also be given to Liz Greig, formerly of Dundee University, who has always been an extremely important protagonist for us, particularly for the way in which her forensic analytical skills have continued to help us to recognise where we need to go next and suggest ways in which this could be possible.

An important expression of thanks must also go to Eileen McKenzie, our administrative support, who has been very patient in her support of us in the collections of the chapters and putting the manuscript together for submission.

Introduction

Why this book?

Pat Wharton and Liz Greig

This book emerged from an invitation to write a second edition of our first book *An Encounter with Reggio Emilia: Children's Early Learning Made Visible*. This we will still do in accordance with its original purpose. This was to share with others the 'why' and 'how' of our decision to implement the Reggio Emilia approach to children's early learning into early years thinking and practice within Stirling Council and our initiation into it. We now felt that we had a different purpose, which was to say in some detail what has been understood since 2008 and that a new book would be the most appropriate context in which to do this. It was important also that this should be said through the voices of children, educators and people, sometimes external to the early years settings, who have collaborated together in developing both a complementary and collective understanding of what it means to work with pedagogical documentation. The book's subtitle reflects this.

Within the chapters of this book the authors will reveal what it has meant for them working with this approach within their respective early years settings. Each of them brings a different perspective, focusing on those aspects of implementing this approach that has made most impact on them through differing roles, different aspects of the practice but most of all through their collaboration with each other and most importantly with the children. In writing these chapters they are not only representing their own experiences and perspectives but also those of their colleagues. They have contributed to this book with some trepidation but in the hope that it might be helpful to others who are in the process of embracing pedagogical documentation.

In Chapter 1, Yvonne and Karen refer to their exciting journey post-2008, and how they have learned to recognise and understand how crucial it is to live the values and principles of this approach to unlock the potential of young children. They also refer to how, in embracing pedagogical documentation it is also necessary to live with its uncertainty; in other words – as they say – 'there is no blueprint', only the one that is created within the respective settings. What they have captured is the ability of this approach to generate and sustain the various vibrant and diverse interests of the children, educators and families. Importantly, they lay great emphasis on professional development opportunities they accessed to support their developing understandings of pedagogical documentation.

In Chapter 2, Sharron gives an honest account of the struggles of herself and her fellow educators to grasp and understand how to engage with a Learning Group in a way that was meaningful to the children, educators and families. What she has managed to relay to the reader is not only some of the challenges that they encountered on the way but also the learning that emerged from their collaboration with the children, families and others who were external to the setting. She has recorded this in a way that reveals the importance of learning to 'really listen to children', and at the same time to recognise their capability to use their talents to support others, including the adults. Sharron has also reflected on the power of pedagogical documentation to engage the parents in a project because of its visibility and the excitement that was generated by the children. A reminder here that this chapter is about being open to a paradigm shift that can cause those involved to feel vulnerable, but at the same time being willing to 'give it a go'.

In Chapter 3, Annie and Lorna recount a project, 'Light and Dark', which has proved to be cathartic for them. For, although they had been involved in a couple of long-term projects before this project was extraordinary in that it gained a momentum that they had never experienced before. Staff and children collaborated together in driving this project forward, first one leading and then the other. All staff, but particularly new staff, were at times mesmerised by the pace of it and the sometimes unexpected places it went to. For example, when some of the children decided that they wanted to research hibernation, when the project had 'seemed' to be trying to answer the question 'where do shadows come from'. This was children connecting their learning in a way that staff teams had not expected and which continued to happen throughout the project. This caused staff halfway through to conduct some research of their own on its possible spontaneity and whether there were ways of specifically encouraging it. They also encountered and have recorded the joyfulness with which the children engaged with the project, none more so than when they realised that they were to become authors and when they discovered the animation software. Joyfulness: a sometimes forgotten element in any dialogue about children's learning.

In Chapter 4, Jackie and Wendie provide a narrative about their pedagogista role in supporting the ongoing implementation and development of pedagogical documentation into usual practice across early years settings in Stirling Council. These roles were put in place to support the sustainability of this approach, which Linda refers to in her chapter. What they give is a very personal perspective on their role and a focus on how they have come to see that changes, and at times discontinuities, can have positive outcomes despite sometimes their perceptions and those of others being completely the opposite. The authors really want to reveal also that it was one child in particular being confronted with similar changes and deriving positives from it that tuned them into the positives in their own situation. Throughout they record how they see themselves as leaving traces and threads of their expertise in supporting pedagogical documentation across early years settings that they support. They hypothesise that these are woven together at times into a rich tapestry and at others left hanging to be connected when another thread of understanding occurs. They suggest that the Japanese Bora serves as a good metaphor for how they see their role making an impact.

Brian reveals in Chapter 5 how an artist has been able to make a really significant impact on the implementation and development of pedagogical documentation across early years settings and some primary schools in Stirling. He very clearly outlines his role in supporting 'Ways of Seeing', which has been able to support staff in making the children's learning visible in a much more powerful way than previously. His influence across all areas of his artistic expertise has been referred to in other chapters, which shows how he has been a significant contributor to the development of a collective understanding of pedagogical documentation. He has also given an important visibility to the multi-perspectival aspect of learning that is embedded in the Reggio Emilia approach to children's learning. The importance of bringing in expertise from other disciplines cannot be underestimated since it brings another perspective to the setting which gives staff, children and families another 'way of seeing.'

In Chapter 6, Sharon and Wendie share their insights into the use of technology to make children's learning visible. For them the new and emerging technologies have been able to provide different dimensions to the way in which we can record children's learning. What they have shared with us is how, by learning to identify children's significant learning, staff have been able to reduce the number of photographs taken. Previously, images taken were prolific until staff understood to take only those that had a significance for the child at a particular moment in time. They are in thrall to the diversity of these technologies and the speed with which they are emerging on an almost monthly basis. They give really potent examples, not only of how children quickly learn to use them, but also how they are being used by staff to reveal the learning and the characteristics of children in a more detailed way: for example, using video clips of a sequence with a child, aspects of which would not have been known through a photograph. Another very powerful example of the use of the camera is when it has been used by a child in one of the settings as his voice, in fact, to provoke him to speak in the nursery, which he had never done before. In agreement with the Stirling University research paper, they also present a more positive view of technology and its use by children. Together, they provide a counter message to the one current in the media whose dominant theme tends to be that children's use of technology has a negative impact on other parts of their lives.

Tanya tells in Chapter 7 of her experience of taking Pedagogical Documentation into the primary school setting. She very clearly describes how she and her colleagues in the nursery and the school have negotiated this, highlighting the importance of shared professional dialogue sessions between nursery and school staff teams to decide on how to integrate this approach into a school setting. What they choose as the integration tool is a joint project that travels with the children from the nursery setting into the school. Tanya takes us into the classroom and reveals the methodology she and her colleague used in another classroom to embed pedagogical documentation into usual school practice. Whilst she is clear about the challenges she is also very clear about how it is positively impacting on the children's learning and the staff in the school.

Working with pedagogical documentation: collective and current understandings

Current and collective understandings: what are they?

Values and principles

First and foremost it means being committed to living the values and principles of this approach within everyday practice. This means really listening to children, respecting their thoughts, ideas and theories, always working with the child as capable and competent, and collaborating with them in a spirit of reciprocal learning and interaction. Sometimes adults and children exchange roles, sometimes the children being the teachers while at others times learning from and with the adult. Children co-researching alongside adults and parents, this always being a key feature of any interest being pursued, emerging as a collaborative approach to children's early learning. Staff have made it a priority to live these values and principles, knowing that these are key to the dynamic that helps children, staff and others to empower this approach. The values and principles have become a continuing focus for staff teams through professional dialogue on a regular basis and are a crucial part of any induction procedures for new members of staff.

> Values are the ideals that a person aspires to in his or her life. These values act as a point of reference in our judgments and our conduct, and on this basis we conform (or not) our relationships within the social group of reference (community, social, culture). Values define cultures and are one of the foundations on which society is based.
>
> *C. Rinaldi quoted in Giudici et al. 2001, 39*

Belief in pedagogical documentation

It means having a belief in pedagogical documentation as a way of unlocking the potential of children and adults as they collaborate with each other in a rich exchange of ideas and creative thinking. The importance of the visibility of children's learning – the strategies, skills, and processes they use in their enquiries across an increasing range of media, cameras, videos, written narratives, folders, flip cameras, tablets, big LCD screens etc. – within the settings has really been more deeply understood by us, because it reminds all those connected to the children of their current learning but also provides the opportunity to revisit, evaluate and extend it. It has also meant that families have been more willing to engage with it because it is there and the children are keen to share their learning and interest with them. The power of following the interests of the children to inspire learning that it is meaningful to them is accepted and embedded in practice. As is the understanding that every interest can continue to live because of its visibility and always has the possibility to be regenerated or extended by the same or new generations of children coming into the setting who can offer different perspectives. What has also been realised is the important part that meaningful provocations can play in sometimes regenerating an interest that seems to have run its course.

Learning about learning

If we are to make children's early learning visible, it also must mean that we must have a good understanding of what learning can look and feel like and the complexities of it. It has been our experience that we have really had to consider what our understandings are and to go deeper into what learning is and how to recognise and record it. Coming to terms with a lack of understanding about the theories of development and learning and the strategies, processes and skills of learning has been a surprise to all those involved since there was a view that we knew it all. However, as we have delved deeper, to our consternation we have discovered that maybe we did not know it as well as we thought. This knowledge prompted us to organise and present courses on this, which have been helpful in our search to make meaning of the complexity of learning and how to recognise when it is significant for individual children, which of course depends on that combined knowledge of understanding what learning can look like and knowing the child as a whole person. This is an area we continue to work on and we suspect will need to be ongoing as we go deeper with our research into learning and its complexities.

> Learning is subjective, complex, cannot be mandated and needs us to reinterpret our role, becoming researchers in practice rather than all knowing teachers.
>
> *Sully 2006, 13*

Professional dialogue

It means continuing to invest in professional dialogue encounters within and beyond staff teams, and seeing these as a necessity so that understandings about children and their learning can be deepened and therefore supported more effectively. Time to make sure this happens has remained an issue but is nevertheless understood as a driver in the pursuit of implementing pedagogical documentation into practice. How to do this is always under discussion, invented and sometimes reinvented. Pedagogistas can often be the provocateurs in such exchanges because of their dedicated role within a setting that is not distracted by routine or administrative concerns. To support this there is a Reggio Emilia-inspired network, Joint Encounters, which provides a means for early years settings within a particular locality to share their documentation and aspects of practice that they may currently be struggling with. These are found to be helpful because of the opportunity they provide to devote this time to practice issues and not practical routine matters that can dominate such meetings within an early years setting. Ongoing professional development programmes, which have incorporated such models as external courses, in-house approaches and access to a three-unit Module on Pedagogical Documentation have been and continue to be rich with professional dialogue opportunities to which, over time, staff have been more willing to contribute with growing confidence. Within such professional discourses it is understood that developing a culture of critical enquiry can be key to how we collaborate to improve practice and develop a shared understanding of how we can support each other in our research into pedagogical documentation and its implementation. Embedding such a culture into an early years setting can become a vital self-evaluation tool that is fundamental to pursuing an ongoing commitment to a continuing improvement philosophy within the setting.

> Dialogue is of absolute importance. It is an idea of dialogue not as an exchange but as a process of transformation where you lose absolutely the possibility of controlling the final result. And it goes to infinity, it goes to the universe, you can get lost. And for human beings nowadays, and for women particularly, to get lost is a possibility and a risk, you know?
>
> *Rinaldi 2006, 1*

Importance of language

It means we have realised the importance of language in our ongoing exchanges with each other. Usage of language can have the ability at times to restrict our responses to certain aspects of our work. For example, we have interrogated the word ' planning', which has become part of our everyday language and wondered how we interpret it in terms of what it can commit us to in our usual practice. The outcome of such scrutiny has led us to understand that it could have had a restrictive effect on how we work because there can be an inclination to keep to any plan made because it has been made and not because it is necessarily serving the best interests of the children it is meant to be supporting. This has led us to consider other words or terms that could give a flexibility to our approach in supporting children's learning. Terms like 'proposals for learning' and 'possibilities for learning' are now being used much more widely within Stirling Council. We think these are much more responsive terms in relation to the pursuits of children's interests wherever this takes them and frees staff from 'plans' that often are created in advance and take no account of the rhizomatic nature of learning. Reforming the language can mean reforming our approach to how we support children's learning. Another example is how researchers and co-researchers have become part of the vocabulary of both educators and children when they are engaging in the development of an interest and finding information through several mediums that are available to them. We are also deepening our conversations with children and families, which encourages both to use the language of learning when discussing the child's progress in the setting. Questions that open this out with young children are continually under discussion amongst individual staff teams and also in collaboration with other staff teams when opportunities arise for this to happen.

Organisation of the setting

It means that we need to look at the organisation of the setting and give serious consideration to the routines we have in place. We need to ask ourselves to what extent do routines within our settings support children's early learning. Do they contribute to the life of the setting in a way that allows children to follow a seam of learning, or do they obstruct learning because they have to be adhered to. To ensure that the former is the case the routines should and must be under ongoing review so each generation of children coming into the setting have access to routines that put 'children first'. The voices of children and families need to be heard alongside those of educators within such reviews because such a collaboration can result in routines being established which reflect and support the needs and aspirations of all the collaborators. In the same vein educators have increasingly understood what it means to create an environment, indoors and outdoors, that gives priority to space and resources that are attractive, multi-dimensional and which have a strong natural influence. We have understood the term 'the environment is the third teacher' and its significance in creating an atmosphere where children are expected to be curious and explore and 'to be' with people who invite them to collaborate with them in search of new meanings and new learning. Pursuing such aims, the space within the setting indoors and outdoors becomes a mutual and reciprocal meeting place where all are welcomed to participate in an adventure taking them to who knows where!

Visibilities of learning

Pedagogical documentation as content is material which records what the children are saying and doing, the work of the children ... for example handwritten notes of what is said and done, audio and video recordings, still images, computer graphics, children's work itself ... This material makes the pedagogical work concrete and visible (audible), as such it is an important ingredient for the process of documentation.

Dahlberg, Moss and Pence 1999, 47

It means that we have understood the importance of making children's early learning transparent across a range of visibilities since this has meant that different audiences – e.g. children, families and people external to the settings – respond to different stimuli. This has been made apparent to us when we have noticed, for example, the impact of LCD screens in accessing both families and children to visibilities of their learning. This has had the effect of supporting children's evaluation of their own work and deciding where they might want to go next in their research of a particular interest. In addition, this visibility has provided an incentive to families to support the interest at home or in some cases to become actively involved within the setting. Other visibilities, such as folders strategically placed have been successful with another group of families and some of them have made contributions to these folders that were contrary to previous connections with their children's work in the setting. Dynamic images via photographs or video clips of the children active in the setting have also been significant for children in seeing themselves in a very positive way and in alerting their families to their capabilities. All of these visibilities and others like PowerPoint presentations have been thoughtfully tried out over the years since there has been a recognition that to do so means that children's learning will reach a wider audience both within the education community and beyond.

Of course, what we have also needed to pay attention to in constructing those visibilities that require a text is that the intention should be to reveal and make transparent the children's significant learning and conceptual understandings in the foreground and the context and experiences in the background, always being aware that brevity will draw an audience rather than density. This is an area that we would still consider very much to be work in progress and has been, and will continue to be, the subject of much professional dialogue within and outside Professional Development courses.

National curriculum guidance

What it also means is that, as in other parts of the UK and beyond, we have curriculum guidance known as Curriculum for Excellence, which we also have to take account of in our work with young children. However, we are fortunate in one respect in that the values and principles of this merge very well with those of pedagogical documentation. What can be problematic are other aspects of the guidance for implementation, which have posed possible contradictions to our own approach through pedagogical documentation. We have researched ways of accommodating both and we feel that we have achieved a degree of success with this, which has been recognised very positively by inspection teams from the regulation organisation in Scotland. How we have come to this is important to record since we have always known that we would continue to work with pedagogical documentation but that we would also need to not only convince others of its powerful way of reflecting children's capabilities but also make it clear at the same time that we are acknowledging the curriculum guidance within our ways of recording.

Uncertainty: What can it mean? What can it feel like?

For those of us involved with the implementation of this approach it has meant living with uncertainty. It can be an unfortunate truth that educators and others working with children can prefer to work from a prescriptive set of guidance that they think if they follow they 'are getting it right'. This is referred to it in Yvonne's and Karen's chapter when they say 'there is no blueprint'. It is entirely understandable that we do not want to 'get it wrong', but when working with pedagogical documentation it is crucial that we develop an entirely different mind-set that accommodates uncertainly because we cannot predict which interests of the children will emerge and where their learning will take them. This means that we need to respond, on occasions spontaneously, from a position of not being prepared, which at times feels uncomfortable because we are not confident in our knowledge base about certain topics that children choose to engage with.

> Maintain a readiness to change points of views so as never to have too many certainties.
>
> *Malaguzzi* et al. *1987*

Children knowing more about topics can also feel undermining for staff because they may feel a loss of control over the direction that it appears to be taking. This can make them question their own abilities when in a more 'certain way' of operating they felt in control. A member of staff said to me recently, following courses she had been involved with 'I am now able to embrace interests that the children suggest, knowing now that in collaboration with them I will learn more about it from them and through my own research I will be able to contribute to it as well. I am accepting that the child can teach me.' There have been many conversations with staff teams regarding this underlying uncertainty that at times seems to envelop them. They are struggling sometimes to find a way forward with particular aspects of the lived values, like finding the time to listen in depth to children's voices in a busy day and at times with particular practice issues such as the requirement of staff to be flexible in support of a particular development in relation to an episode or project that is emerging. At other times their desire for certainty can overtake them when they notice in dialogue with educators from other settings that they are making children's learning visible in ways different to their own. In such situations we have found it important to remind staff that a different approach to this does not mean it is wrong, it means that in difference we can find richness because each setting constructs their visibilities in accordance with the individuality of children and of the staff members, as well as the context and locality of the respective settings. It is also in such engagements and within professional development situations that we encourage staff to converse always in the language of the possible rather than in the language of the definitive. A troublesome area of uncertainty can also arise for staff when trying to accommodate pedagogical documentation and national guidance, mentioned earlier in this chapter, because they feel under pressure when an inspection looms. Encouraging staff to have courage in articulating the convergence of one approach with the other has been part of an ongoing discourse that is proving to have an effect because, as mentioned earlier, inspection teams are recognising the relationship between the two and have been happy in the knowledge that children's learning is being made visible and for their purposes made accountable through pedagogical documentation. However, we are beginning to see that living with uncertainty and eventually winning through can be a driver for change and that over time, working through its painful process can have the effect of making us not only more thoughtful about how we collaborate with children and families, but also much more responsive and able to make a real difference to children's lives. We continue to travel with hope!

> This means seeing uncertainty and dissensus as possibilities not dangers, and an openness to being surprised and finding new meanings. As teachers, we have to carry out this role (as co-constructors) in full awareness of our vulnerability, and this means accepting doubts and mistakes as well as allowing for surprise and curiosity, all of which are necessary for true acts of knowledge and creation.
>
> *C. Rinaldi quoted in Dahlberg and Moss 2005, 104*

Chapter 1

Current perspectives

Karen McLaughlin and Yvonne Thomson

The purpose of this chapter is to share with the reader our own reflections and thoughts as a team on how our knowledge and understanding of pedagogical documentation has evolved. It has now been six years since the pilot nurseries documentation informed *An Encounter with Reggio Emilia Children's Early Learning Made Visible*. A few members of the core team from Doune Nursery were delighted to come together to reflect on the subsequent development of how we made children's early learning visible.

Through our recent reflections we believe that there were many factors and influences that contributed to our team's deeper understanding, knowledge, progression, confidence and the implementation of the documentation approach to early learning into early years practice. For most of the past decade the team remained constant with little staff change. This was most helpful in consolidating, progressing and developing this pedagogical approach. We will discuss further aspects of these important factors including: what we record, our questioning skills, formation of learning groups, consultation, observation, assessment, planning, identifying a sustained interest, family and community involvement, publication of documentation and children's rights. We strongly believe that relationships with children, families, staff, other professionals nationally and internationally as well as creative artists have been central to developing our understanding of pedagogical documentation with all stakeholders working together to provide a rich, motivating, fun, varied, challenging and exciting learning environments for children, families and staff.

The main focus of documentation presented in the first edition was an extract from the 'Light and Dark' Learning Group. At this point as a team we still felt that we were on a journey of discovery; we still are! Although we took tentative steps learning and implementing our understandings of documenting children's learning it was an exciting, challenging and thought-provoking time. At this time the documentation process involved us in taking lots of photographs, video footage and transcribing a large quantity of children's and educators dialogue resulting in recording many episodes of children engaging in exploratory experiences. What we have since understood is that we should restrict ourselves to capturing significant learning and events across a range of media, which is both more meaningful and more manageable across the setting. As a team we regularly reflected and evaluated our documentation and began to change how we recorded children's learning experiences. Through analysis of our pedagogical documentation it was decided to record the educator's role, responses and conversations with children as a tool for self-reflection. This evidence enabled us to identify how to further develop our skills when posing questions to children. Our questions became more considered and open ended, which provoked more detailed responses from the children. To support staff's deeper understanding of the documentation approach we developed a bank of questions. Examples include:

- How are the team planning for children's learning in a cohesive, progressive, relevant and meaningful way, taking account of individual children's interest?
- How are we actively encouraging motivation and promoting a culture of enquiry and critical thinking?
- How are we actively encouraging, maximising and supporting children's active learning, participation, collaboration and working with others?

These are questions we continue to reflect upon and seek to answer. The evidence we gathered from such specific questioning of ourselves and a range of documentation including children's individual planning (see examples below) enabled us to assess children's learning, plan progressions in children's learning and identify that experiences in which children were engaging required to be progressed from individual interests to in-depth learning group experiences. Children's individual planning of their own learning experiences was developed and implemented into practice over a period of time. Through such a system children are invited to plan for their own learning experiences, graphically representing their choices. Educators support and scaffold children through conversations that encourage and enable children to make visible their own learning. Through skilful interactions and observations educators identify and record children's individual interests, and learning intentions.

Through the development of our Learning Group meetings we recognised and developed a format to Learning Groups, which enabled us to embed a Learning Group culture into our daily practice. The formation of Learning Groups developed through observation of a group of children who were developing a shared interest over a period of time, sharing their knowledge, ideas, information, resources from home and nursery, and fun experiences to extend their understanding of their favourite topics. We recognised the importance of the environment to hold Learning Group consultations in smaller groups in a quieter space. This ensured children were having the opportunity to be listened to. During consultation with children we recognised it was necessary for some children to have the opportunity to have extended time for their responses, which in turn allowed for more thoughtful answers when sharing their own theories and opinions. This also helped developed their questioning skills as well as further promoted self-confidence to speak out loud with their peers. All children would be invited to attend a Learning Group meeting to discuss a particular interest, e.g. space, dinosaurs, dance, eco schools, castles, building, camera, photography, their community. From our ongoing observations we noted that the children who were actively engaging in experiences relating to the specific interest would independently want to be involved in the children's meeting. The process began with children being supported and encouraged to create a mind map to represent their current knowledge, experiences, feelings or thoughts on the specific area of interest, which led to discussing what they would like to learn next. As the Learning Group developed, both educators and children extended their knowledge base as they researched together.

Examples of children's planning

Isabella asks to do her planning. Isabella points out her learning 'look what I can do ... my mummy told me. What else do I have to do?' Isabella asks about the letters.

'I'm going to do the theatre. I'm going to dress up and dance. I'm going to dance in there and make the music. I'm going to play with that [Isabella draws a bongo drum]. I like them because they make nice sounds.'

Isabella

Sophie planning

Sophie: 'We'll be showing her [visiting professional dancer] the nursery. Maybe do different dancing not just ballet dancing. I'll do some Indian dancing. We'll put some music on, put on a little show for her. I think maybe she'll bring some ballet shoes. We just have ballet dancers' and princess's dresses. I've drawn a picture of Snow White, she's my favourite princess. I was thinking maybe we could have a wee show for her [visiting professional dancer].'

Children opted in and out of the Learning Group depending on the nature of the experiences being explored e.g.: researching information on the internet; exploring fiction and/or non-fiction books; creative art experiences such as drawing, painting, model making with clay; role play or performing to musical experiences; or investigating our local community. Through our deepening understanding of the importance of consulting with children and them understanding how to be consulted we began to understand that how we recorded children's responses – for example through mind maps, voting, children's journals, families' feedback, creative experiences, photographs, videos, children's evaluations of learning and children's audits – would reflect the individual learning processes in varying ways.

Initial Space Learning Group meeting

Through these we were able plan possible learning experiences for children and be more considered in the different ways children explore learning. We became more confident in scaffolding children in their learning, recognising the difference between when children may have truly lost interest in an experience or topic and when it simply required using carefully considered and appropriate provocations to sustain children's interest. Through the Learning Group meetings we were able to identify children's ability to engage in purposeful in-depth conversations, to share their breadth of knowledge and experience with others and to recognise children's individual skills. We also were beginning to understand that children recognised their own learning and that of others. Children discussed their own learning progressions, recognised other children's interests and skills and made visible their enthusiasm for learning and supported and engaged in peer learning situations where it was helpful and appropriate. As children listened to each other's ideas and saw each other's work they had the opportunity to learn that there are different points of view. Through exploring shared interests and listening to different perspectives they expand their understandings.

We continued to be committed to attend regular local authority joint encounters facilitated by Stirling Council's Early Years Team to meet with other educators to further engage, explore, reflect and evaluate each other's interpretation, understanding and developing knowledge of how we were making children's early learning visible. Furthermore, and central to the culture within Doune Nursery, was staff commitment to furthering their own professional development with each member of the staff team engaging in various levels of further study. This generated an ethos of professional dialogue allowing us to implement theoretical perspectives into practice, at the same time taking account of national and curriculum documents, which supported staff to go deeper as professionals in the field of early childhood.

We recognised the importance of national and international perspectives in developing our understanding of the documentation approach. We welcomed many opportunities to engage in professional dialogue with early years educators from around the world including Carlina Rinaldi, Wendy Lee, Patricia McGrath, Sue Dockett and many others that evoked exciting and thought provoking discussions. This type of dialogue allowed us to share our pedagogical documentation approach and also gain the expertise of others with the common link of the value that we place in early years education around the world. We understood more the global impact on children of the way in which we support them in their learning. It reaffirmed that we were all at different stages of the journey with the guiding principles of pedagogical documentation at its heart. In order to develop more understanding of this approach and the history of how it began a few staff members participated in study trips to Reggio Emilia, Italy, generating an excitement in the possibilities that could emerge from personal experience. It proved an excellent opportunity to further enhance existing experience, which deepened our understanding of the documentation approach to early learning, developed further understandings of Reggio Emilia philosophy and practice and enabled engagement with others working in the field of early learning,

Staff meeting

further enhancing our own professional learning and understanding of children as learners and researchers and provoked us to develop further this inspired innovative practice.

Our HM Inspectorate and Care Commission Reports (2011) (National Quality Regulators) further validated our approach grading all areas excellent giving us further validation for working with pedagogical documentation. Through working with this approach the particular strengths that they identified were as follows:

- making available to children a range of quality experiences that liberated their learning;
- in so doing, meeting the learning needs of children both collectively and individually;
- empowering children to take responsibility and be consulted about their own learning pathways;
- children's ability to learn how to be consulted and as a result make appropriate choices about learning and about those aspects of the setting that affected them;
- the capability of the children to be self-assessors of their own learning and development;
- the self-evaluative practice that permeated the everyday life of the nursery;
- the leadership of the head and her commitment to a distributive leadership approach within the nursery setting.

Such validation from a government agency gave us greater confidence to develop our pedagogical documentation practice since we had always retained an element of reservation about how government agencies would view this innovative approach to children's early learning. So with renewed enthusiasm and supported by the vision and strong leadership of the nursery's head we remained fully committed to the pedagogical documentation approach to children's learning. We had a greater understanding of the process and how it needed all the components in place to make it work, which meant all staff were learning together and alongside the children, offering their particular expertise, which included ICT creativity and the growing ability to hold meaningful conversations with the children and each other. What we were also coming to terms with was the uncertainty that working with this approach brought, since there was and is not a blueprint that can be referred to and followed. We make our own blueprints and where they can be helpful we share them with others.

As a team we were encouraged to adopt a more distributive approach to leading Learning Groups. Educators were given autonomy and responsibility to take forward and lead their own Learning Group, with support given from the nursery's head.

As the years progressed and our understandings grew and developed we began refining more of what we were recording, taking into account our audiences in-house, locally and nationally. Various ways of presenting included providing a narrative that made the learning visible without the experience dominating the text and understanding the importance of limiting the text to essential information supported with pertinent photographs highlighting significant learning. This led to taking fewer photographs and through staff development with artist Brian Hartley (see Chapter 5) we became better skilled at taking more powerful images and recognised the advancement of ICT equipment to enhance our recording of children's learning.

Our family and community engagement with pedagogical documentation progressed. As part of the nursery induction, individual family skills and experiences were identified from the onset. Families worked in partnership with us sharing their skills and knowledge to deepen children's experiences. Participation extended to include siblings, buddies from school, teachers, grandparents and other specialists to further support the children's learning. The strong partnership between the nursery, families and wider community enabled the development of a learning group culture with all stakeholders working together to provide a rich, motivating, fun, exciting learning environment in which everybody was understood as a learner. Family participation and evaluations became central to our approach.

Space Learning Group – Participation with Primary 6 Children

When Flynn's granddad came to pick him up at the end of the session, the children were excited to tell him about the meeting and the story of Peppa Pig's grandfather having a telescope. The children asked Flynn's granddad if he had a telescope. He told the children that although he didn't have a telescope he did actually once work alongside the astronaut 'Ox' Van Hoffman. Flynn's granddad said he would try and find some photographs of his friend the astronaut for Flynn to bring to nursery to share with his friends.

Doune primary 6 children join the nursery Space Learning Group to share their knowledge and learn about space

Family evaluation

The children are so full of enthusiasm! So many of the children are interested in rockets and space travel ... This has great links to your eco schools work and how we need to protect our world ... It is so important that we educate and inform our youngest children of how to protect our earth.

Parents had regular opportunities to view their child's learning documentation through individual journals, curriculum planning, creativity events, video displays, parent's evenings, newspaper features and through contributing to their child's individual learning journals.

Another visibility of documentation produced was a CD rom gifted to families at the end of their nursery experience capturing their child's learning journey. A childrens art gallery was created within the nursery placing high value on children's creative talents. The gallery makes visible children's ideas, and values and respects children's representations and celebrates children's achievements with families and the wider community.

In order to make the documentation approach more visible in the local community staff created book publications through an internet resource called Blurb, documenting a range of Learning Groups with one of the publications being added to the local library and made available to borrow. One of these was a book entitled *Children's Rights*, which made visible within the nursery, to parents and the wider community how we upheld the rights of the child.

A Parent's Guide to Stirling Council's Documentation Approach was written by Marian Kayes, the former Head of Doune Nursery, to share with other families what a documentation approach to early learning can look like for families and their children. Threaded throughout the guide is valued feedback from parents, families, children, the team and HMIE, who have shared their perspectives and experiences of the documentation approach to learning.

Children's Gallery

Fundamental to this way of working was the recognition of children as citizens of today with democratic rights enshrined in law (United Nations Convention on the Rights of the Child). The guiding principles of Reggio Emilia informed our vision of the children being competent, rich and resourceful and proved integral and central to this way of working.

> Reggio Emilia Approach is an educational philosophy based on the image of the child and of human beings as possessing strong potentials for development and as a subject of rights who learns and grows in the relationships with others.
>
> *Reggio Children Identity, www.reggiochildren.it*

Article 12 of the United Nations Convention on the Rights of the Child (UNCRC) declares that children have the right to say what they think should happen when adults are making decisions that affect them, and to have their opinions taken into account (UNICEF). Empowering children to have their views listened to and respected is at the core of our nursery practice. Children's views were actively sought, recorded, respected, valued and acted upon. The children's active participation and consultation helped shape the nursery's environment, ethos and culture and allowed for children to influence their own learning. In 2011 the nursery was recognised and rewarded the UNICEF UK Rights Respecting Schools Award.

What have we learned since our 'Light and Dark' project (previous book 2008)

The documentation approach to learning is a journey that varies across culture and respective early years settings, even within the same local council area. The principles of the approach serve as a guide but the combination of those involved in each recorded experience – the children, the educators, families, community and culture – create an outcome that is unique to those who participate in the process. We have learned there is no 'right' or 'wrong' way to document children's learning; each setting will have identified strategies, which they believe encapsulate children's early learning processes, underpinned by the values and principles of pedagogical documentation.

Educators understood that we could not be experts in all the subjects in which children were interested, but came to enjoy learning together with (and, in some cases, from) the children. Cohesive team-working and a willingness to continue to develop an understanding of pedagogical documentation as an ongoing process is essential in developing our implementation of it. Guided always by the values and principles of pedagogical documentation we increasingly have come to know how important it is to listen to the voice of the child and make it visible in diverse ways so that it can reach all audiences, and in such forums it can be celebrated, shared, heard and understood.

The importance of time also became apparent during our journey. We came to understand that this is a process that cannot be rushed; time must be given in the first instance to identify learning that can be explored and expanded. Time must also be given for children to consolidate their experiences and revisit their learning to support their metacognitive processes. Trying to record too many experiences becomes unmanageable and the experiences can lose value and meaning. Often a powerful photograph was more able to convey the learning that was taking place.

The future

> What we are talking about is not the application of some finalized model, universal in scope and definitive in nature, but rather the adoption of a process of questioning, dialogue, reflection and meaning making which leads we know not where and has no obvious end point: it is work continuously in progress.
>
> *Cited in Rinaldi 2013, 61*

Chapter 2

An engagement with the Learning Group process

Sharron McIntosh

A Learning Group is a collection of persons emotionally, intellectually and aesthetic-ally engaged in solving problems, creating products, and making meaning – an assemblage in which each person learns autonomously and through the ways of learning of others.

Krechevsky 2001, 285

Approximately thirteen years ago, Park Drive Nursery in Stirling piloted the documentation approach to children's learning. I consider myself very fortunate to have been part of the process from the outset, and to have worked in partnership with children and staff on several Learning Group projects. With each episode of learning came a deeper understand-ing of the documentation process; the ways in which our roles as educators and the children's learning are inextricably linked and the way documentation becomes a powerful visibility of children trying to make sense of their world. To try and capture the essence of what was important to us as an establishment, our growth and development as educators and our understanding of the relationship between pedagogical documentation and Learn-ing Groups is not an easy task, as so many factors and influences have impacted on our practice during that time. In this chapter I hope to take you on our journey; to try to illus-trate how significant Learning Group encounters have changed our thinking in terms of:

- understanding what a Learning Group is about and what our roles are within the group;
- really listening to children with all of our senses;
- recognising the importance of listening to and seeing the connections children make to their experiences and their own knowledge and understanding of their world – how they have made meaning;
- recognising the importance of parental involvement in a Learning Group;
- understanding what a Learning Group is about and what our roles could be within the group.

In the beginning, our experience of Learning Groups was theoretical. We may have thought that we understood the concept, but in reality we had little or no practical experience of the

Learning Group process for educators and children alike and did not understand that it is subjective, open to different interpretation and is, in fact, multi-dimensional.

Having worked alongside another colleague on a mural within a loosely structured adult-led project mentioned in previous book (L. Kinney, P. Wharton 2008) we were eager to embark upon another project.

We attempted to develop three other Learning Groups, all of which 'fizzled out' fairly quickly because we were unable to sustain the children's interest in the topic. However, just at the point when we were beginning to feel disheartened a series of events came together that changed our whole perception of the Learning Group process and our roles as educators side by side with the children.

We were invited to be part of an Action Research project funded by Bernard Van Leer that was to focus on Learning Groups. This coincided with the nursery acquiring a beautiful wall hanging from a local further education college, which we thought might be a provocation for the children and might just spark an interest that could ignite into a project. Interestingly, the parents paid more attention to it initially than the children, with the parents drawing their children into conversations about it (one of these parents subsequently became a member of the Learning Group). Together with my colleague we developed this conversation further with the children in the art and craft area that we were supporting at that time. Visits to the wall hanging followed and soon we noticed that collage work was being created that seemed to have been inspired by the wall hanging. Encouraged by our Early Childhood Link Officer and the person leading the Action Research project a group of six children emerged showing a real interest in making a wall hanging of their own. What was explained to the children was that it would be helpful if together we put forward suggestions about what our wall hanging could look like and how we could find out how to create it. At this point we were 'playing with possibilities' and were very much of a mind to 'see what happened' because for all of us it was a leap in the dark. The first thing the children wanted to do was to give it a name and they were very enthused by the idea that they were a Learning Group. They called their project 'This is Gonna Be Fun' (Seascape) because they sensed that it was going to be so (Seascape).

As educators we were very clear that we wanted to ensure that this Learning Group would be a positive experience for the children and the educators who were keen to capture the learning effectively. We were soon to discover that documentation is not just a way of recording learning, it also creates an emotional bond between itself, the child and the documenter.

To support this emerging project it was decided that two educators (myself and Lynne) would lead the Learning Group with other educators in the setting playing a supporting role. At this early stage we had yet to understand and define the roles that children would play in this process. However Matthew, a member of the Learning Group, soon gave us a clear lead on this. I was trying in vain to multitask: to transcribe the conversation whilst at the same time taking photographs, doing my best to support the parent in her role and managing the crowd of children who had gathered to join in or just to watch. Noticing my less than perfect efforts, Matthew asked, 'Will I take the photographs Sharron?' This was agreed and from then on his role was as photographer of the group – the image of the child as rich and resourceful became real in my eyes. We now had educators, children and parents in a process of defining their role within the Learning Group, fundamental to this being their desire to be a key part of it.

Members of learning groups include adults as well as children.

Krechevsky 2001, 286

We were supported through the process of research, investigation and discovery by the Action Researcher whose input as a critical friend became vital to our ongoing understanding of the Learning Group process. I must confess that the feelings of walking in blind were sometimes overpowering and the thought of our practice being 'under scrutiny' gave us more than a little anxiety. However, we were committed to the approach and embraced the experience wholeheartedly, if not with a little trepidation. The spiral of learning that we embarked upon during this project was rivalled only by the satisfaction that we received from feeling that at last we were documenting a Learning Group with a modicum of success. The project spanned an entire year and to truly reflect its impact would be impossible in one chapter. I will therefore focus on a few key elements that have been significant in supporting us with our future involvements with subsequent learning group projects.

Really listening to the children with all of our senses

As educators we learned to really listen to the children as we made decisions by involving them in the processes involved in the development of the Seascape. What this looked like in practice was that the children were consulted about the design of the Seascape as well as the selection of materials that were used in its ongoing development. In the beginning we saw this simply as a collage until the children raised important questions about fundamental elements connected to it, which began to change our understanding of possibilities that could emerge from within this Learning Group. For example, when a parent brought in an orange floral fabric one of the children asked 'Was this for the sea?'. Both my colleague and myself stopped and listened, realising the implications of this question and what we were beginning to understand about listening to the children and responding by posing the appropriate question, which at this time was 'Have you been to the sea?'. Previously we might have answered giving them the facts about the sea. Instead we entered into a conversation with them that revealed that before we could consider representing the sea on the collage we would need to engage in a piece of research about the sea, its colour and its properties. Our own understanding of the importance of asking open-ended questions was beginning to emerge.

We were also beginning to see the Seascape not only as important for itself but more importantly as a scaffold on which to develop and hang the children's learning. Thus began our transition from a group of adults and children to co-constructors of theories, investigators, researchers and scientists with the roles of educators and children as learners becoming intertwined. One important outcome of this was that questions that arose and resulting problems that needed to be solved did not remain in the nursery. They also were taken home to the families, which sometimes resulted in more questions being brought back to the core Learning Group. One such occasion was when one child came to the Learning Group the next morning to say, 'I have another problem to solve. Sometimes when the water comes out of the tap very fast, it's white.' Clearly both in the nursery and at home they were still puzzling over the different colours water appeared to have in different situations. The atmosphere within the group in these early days of investigation and experimentation was electric. This question led the group to extend their research further into the sea and water. The educators proposed to the children that they should engage in some experiments with water to which one child responded. 'What is an experiment?' One question was leading to another!

> The focus of learning in learning groups extends beyond the learning of individuals to create a collective body of knowledge.
>
> *Ibid., 286*

This led us to realise the importance of listening to and seeing the connections children make through their own experiences and their knowledge and understanding of the world – how they make meaning. What we understood now was that the children were trying to make sense of why water appeared to be different colours when they encountered it in different situations. A series of experiments about water followed, very tentatively conducted within the nursery setting. Then it was decided that, once the children had noticed that the colour of water when coming fast out of the tap was white, this needed further exploration.

As part of this exploration we decided to visit a local waterfall, including the outdoors in our experimentation. Once again, this led us to be reminded of our own limitations. We consistently doubted ourselves and what we were doing and we made many mistakes. I recall with some discomfort part of what followed. On our return from the waterfall, as part of the documenting process, we gave the children white A4 paper and blue paint to represent the water at the waterfall which had disappointing outcomes for the children and the educators. The question posed during a professional dialogue session was 'why white paper and blue paint?' Our reason for this was more about expediency than reflective of what resources might be appropriate for this particular experience for the children. Suffice to say the trip to the waterfall was made again and a range of appropriate resources was provided on site. For example, a variety of different colour shapes and sizes of paper, different colours of marking tools and easels on which the children could secure their papers etc. The children painted the waterfall and had the resources at hand to enable them to capture what the waterfall meant to them individually. As the children painted, you could have heard a pin drop over the roaring water and the paintings created were alive with energy.

As educators we realised that this visual experience not only helped the children's understanding of the properties and colour of water but also turned out to be quite a learning curve for ourselves as the educators. The children had been immersed in the aesthetic element of learning and the adults had learned that the environment really is 'the third teacher'. Such a vital and appropriately resourced experience, which allowed the children to represent what they had understood about the colour of water and its relationship with speed and context in a very much more representative way than had the previous visibilities.

What the educators understood from this experience was that because key elements of the process were being documented, we were able to revisit all the experiments, and importantly this particular situation, as an opportunity to try again. In other words our inadequacies became problems to be solved. The children's confidence grew from the knowledge that making mistakes is all part of the learning process and children and adults together embracing the resolution of problems and mistakes made everybody stronger. This experience not only alerted us to the importance of real experiences and associated resources to represent it but also the importance of taking time to stop, watch and see the children's learning through the eyes of the child.

Painting at the waterfall

> Members of the learning groups are engaged in the emotional and aesthetic as well as the intellectual dimensions of learning.
>
> *Ibid.*

It would also be important to mention that whilst there was a core group of children working on this project, other children in the setting knew about the project because it was becoming increasingly visible in the nursery. At times they contributed to the discussions about how to progress the project and at others wanted a 'more hands on' part to play in it; there was such an occasion when a parent was helping the children to create a part of the Seascape. Two children decided that they would attach their own version of an overhanging tree to the wall hanging and when the core group of children learned what they had done there was great consternation because they had not sought their permission. This was another important understanding that we gained about how children's work should be respected and where other children seek to contribute they should first seek the permission of those children who are core to the project.

Around about the same time another salutary experience occurred that really caused us to be thoughtful about how a project led by two members of staff and involving a core group of children can begin to be perceived as exclusive in terms of the rest of the staff team and the parents. We were made aware of this at a professional dialogue session with all staff members in the setting and the Action Researcher. It became clear to all those who were involved with the project that we were not sharing with the whole staff team key elements of the project and what our intentions were. What we realised was that whilst this was not intentional, we had all become so caught up in the excitement and development of the wall hanging that we were not keeping our colleagues up-to-date with it. This was an important realisation because clearly the core group of children were working across the nursery, which involved other members of staff who, whilst wanting to be supportive, felt they did not have sufficient information to be as helpful as they would want to be. This has been another key understanding that has influenced how we have worked with other projects and since this time, as a nursery, we have ensured that at staff meetings updates on any project live at the time are shared with staff teams as well as contributions they may have to make to its development.

Recognising the importance of parental involvement in a Learning Group

The parents became involved in the project at a level that we had never experienced before. Seeing displays and folders of documentation portraying their child's learning and involvement in the project hooked parents into the experience totally. One parent was even prepared to cut up her kitchen table cover to ensure that we were using exactly the right fabric to represent the sea; such was the commitment to the project and to the decisions over which the children had deliberated long and hard. Parents met with lead educators to talk about the project and to learn how the children were responding to their involvement with it and the Learning Group process. What we understood from this was that aspects of the project were being linked with experiences parents were exposing their children to as an extension of what was happening in the nursery, which was further enriching the project and the role that parents were playing within the learning group and at home. 'You know, I listen to my child in a whole different way since we've been part of the learning group' was said to us by one of our Learning Group parents, during 'This is Gonna be Fun' (Seascape) and if anyone still has doubts about the benefits of this approach, I charge you to reflect on the power of the following statement:

> The pleasure of getting together of feeling part of the expectations and future enjoyment that the children will experience is combined with the pleasure of building closer relationships with other parents.

Ibid., 146

Over the course of the next few months we became stronger and stronger as a group and the roles became more defined. Educators, children and parents were equal partners in developing real life skills and a collective body of knowledge and understanding, and all the while we were supported, challenged and encouraged by the Action Researcher.

'This is Gonna be Fun' (Seascape) will always hold a very special place in our hearts since it was transformational in its ability to support our understandings of how Learning Groups can develop and support children's learning not only as a group, but also as individuals. Every Learning Group that I have been involved with since however, has brought something new and different. It has helped to shape our understandings of the Learning Group process and our development as educators in collaboration with children and families.

Seascape completed

Chapter 3

Learning is infectious

Annie Miller and Lorna Willows

In this chapter we have chosen to share with the reader a long-term project that made a significant impact, both professionally and personally, on a whole staff team in Croftamie Nursery in rural Stirling in 2011. It is our hope that in its recounting it reveals how we continue to encounter pedagogical documentation since the project 'The Pakistani Earthquake' featured in *An Encounter with Reggio Emilia: Making Children's Early Learning Visible* in 2008.

The project called 'Light and Dark' started with one of those 'Wow' moments where children had, through use of the overhead projector, discovered their shadows moving on the wall in a special den area of the nursery.[1] The interest and excitement of the children captured the enthusiasm of the educators and together they embarked on an amazing project that was, at times, a 'roller coaster' ride signposting us to many diverse pathways of learning and memorable life experiences. It spanned a whole year and it is our hope that we are able to reflect throughout these pages our amazing discoveries about the learning of children and involved adults as it makes visible how a small Learning Group infected a whole learning community and continues to leave its traces to this day. It was this project and experience that helped us to reach new understandings about working with pedagogical documentation.

The team

Some staff members had been working with pedagogical documentation for approximately twelve years. This group of staff had a wide range of experience, knowledge and skill of this way of working. However, other members of the team were new to the nursery and our way of working and were keen to know how to implement an approach that was entirely new to them. This group of staff needed time to become familiar with the philosophy and pedagogy within the nursery setting, as well as gain knowledge and understanding from experienced team members. These educators struggled to understand the 'right way' to document and make visible children's learning; they needed time to try out, be creative, get into dialogue with colleagues and come to their own realisation that there are many perspectives and answers to the question, 'What is the right way to document?' Staff sometimes find it difficult to grasp that there is no 'right way' until they eventually understand that we are always reaching for ' what is possible' at any given moment in time.

> What is unique about the human species is its dedication to possibility. When we human beings learn, the act of learning carries us beyond what we have encountered and propels us into the realm of the possible.
>
> *Bruner 2011, 10*

It was important that new team members had time to experience, learn about and understand:

- the process of making sense of how to follow children's interests;
- how to provide meaningful and relevant provocations;
- how to ask good questions;
- the importance of really listening to the children;
- how to recognise and capture children's significant learning and make this visible across a range of media forms.

The project – 'Light and Dark'

It all started with a group of children using the overhead projector as a light box. The, 'Wow' moment came when the educator observing the children offered a possibility – an opportunity that may interest, or excite or show new ways of seeing – she flipped the overhead projector up to show the children their shadows projected onto the wall. The children were so amazed they started to dance and jump about exploring with obvious enjoyment and excitement, the movement of their bodies on the wall.

Children were given time and provocations to explore shadows, for example through different mediums, i.e. making a dark room and providing torches, glow sticks (neon), flashing lights and a light projector. The light box was added to the dark room with resources that would encourage the children to explore transparency and opacity.

As the interest in the effects of light and dark grew, the quiet room within the setting became a 'light/dark' room where children could further develop their interest in the overhead projector and mirrors.

What educators observed was the children thinking about and trying to make sense of the features of light, e.g. light shining through, light reflecting back and light being blocked, which they understood caused a shadow.

Educators and children then began to explore shadows and reflections beyond the indoor setting of the nursery to the outdoors in order to deepen their understanding of 'what makes a shadow?' and 'what makes a reflection?'.

The children began to theorise about what they were observing outdoors as they tried to make sense of 'is this my reflection or a shadow in the puddle?' Children began to observe shadows at different times of the day. This led them to ask questions about why shadows move, change shape, change size, disappear and have no detail. They began to look deeper and staff observed this and offered experiences both indoors and outdoors that would help the children in their quest to find answers to their questions.

'Wow, it's magic!'

Exploring and investigating different kinds of light

'If you bend your knees, your reflection copies you'

Capturing courtyard shadows

The Learning Group

Realising that a possible sustainable interest could be developing the staff, through close observations, noticed that it was the same small group of children who seemed more interested in learning about shadows than most of the other children. This group of children were those who were asking lots of questions and were always keen to be involved in any of the experiences being offered around learning about shadows. Educators then discussed with this group of children the opportunity to become a Learning Group, which would focus on finding out about light and dark, including shadows. So that the children were clear about what being a member of a Learning Group could mean it was explained to the children that a Learning Group is a group of people who come together because they share an interest in learning about the same topic, in this case light and dark (shadows). It was also explained to them that in order for the group to together deepen their knowledge and understanding of the shared interest through research and dialogue the following aspects needed to be taken account of and understood.

- It would meet on a regular basis and would make decisions together about what theories and questions to follow up and research.
- Research means, 'finding out more' and that the adults and the children would do this together.
- Adults as well as children would be members of the Learning Group.

Once the children had agreed that they would like to form a Learning Group together the educators, along with the children, constructed a framework that would support it. This included how the educators and children would 'talk' to one another, taking turns, listening to what was being said, asking questions, and that it was okay to disagree with someone and have a different view. The educators role-modelled this for the children and shared examples of good ways and not so good ways of doing this, in order that the children would have a clear framework within which to work.

Having constructed the framework it was then important to agree and allocate tasks to members within the group. The task to take notes was allocated to the two educators who were leading the group. In addition, a child who was known to be skilled with the camera became the photographer through a process of offering this opportunity to the whole group and one child volunteering. It was understood by the group that this role could be shared with other children when they felt confident to undertake it. The group then decided when to meet and the focus of the next meeting.

Provocations

The two educators leading the Learning Group began to think deeply about their allocated roles of posing questions to the children and taking notes. Initially these were some of the questions they asked themselves: 'How can we set up experiences to support learning more about light and dark?' 'Which areas of the nursery indoor and outdoor will provide most opportunities for provocations related to the topic at this stage?' The creative area was their first consideration but then they realised that each area in the setting had the potential to offer appropriate provocations related to light and dark. The example shown below is the provocation of black and white plasticine being left in the creative area, in the hope that children would make connections between the light and dark of shadows.

Educators were disappointed when the children did not initially show an interest in the plasticine, which led to a discussion between them about how best to arouse this. From this the idea emerged that perhaps the children needed an adult to further provoke interactions with the materials, and this they did. One child joined the table with the adult and a dialogue took place around what we could do with the materials. The child decided that she would like to represent her shadow image through the plasticine. During this exchange other children became curious as to what the adult and child were doing and chose to join in. Questions and discussions with children continued around representing from two dimensions to three dimensions and the concept of representing oneself through the plasticine, i.e. form, shape, body, shadow, size and positioning. Children remained interested in this learning and continued to explore model making in this way over a period of weeks, recognising its connection to their interest in light and dark, which the colours of the clay represented (interestingly the learning that took place at this point is revisited and used by children when they come to develop characters for their animation).

Plasticine shadow model

A sub-group emerges

In pursuing some of the various elements of light and dark a sub-group emerged from the core Learning Group who were interested in researching the dark element of light and dark as it affected animals who either only came out in the dark or who hibernated at 'dark times' of the year. This was a very powerful interest with which this group of children really engaged, and through this they developed a real understanding of how light and dark has an effect on how particular creatures responded to these opposing elements of nature. Children's research into this involved them in indoor and outdoor learning. They conducted a number of experiments. For example, they put food that they understood hedgehogs ate outside during the day and kept watch each morning to see if it had been eaten overnight. They dissected owl pellets and through role play practised curling up in a ball so that they could gain an understanding of how those animals felt when they hibernated through autumn into winter. One particular focus that emerged for them was owls, and the staff team felt that inviting an expert into the setting who would bring an owl and who would not only give them detailed information about the life and habitat of an owl, but would also give them a real life experience of an owl would provoke further learning. Prior to his visit the children and staff prepared themselves by conducting as much research as possible about owls through books and the internet. The children were fascinated with this whole experience and Marcus, one of the children in the Learning Group, was so enthused about seeing a real owl that over a period of time, following the visit of the expert, he created a wonderful painted canvas of an owl that hung proudly, first in the nursery and later that year at an early years' exhibition in Stirling to celebrate pedagogical documentation (see plate section).

It was not only Marcus that was enthused; so were a number of parents. One of them who was present was so inspired by what the children were learning that the family took their child camping to see if they could locate one of these animals who preferred the dark to the light. The family documented this and it became part of the overall documentation of the project. Two other parents were particularly interested because they had jobs that related particularly to the hibernation research. One parent was a forestry ranger and he knew the owl expert and it was through this contact that he came into the nursery. Another of the parents worked in a similar job and he brought in the owl pellets and bones from which the children were able to deconstruct and discover what the owl had been feeding on.

The learning becomes contagious

It happened that another group of children in the nursery were pursuing another interest, which was a new computer software package called 'I Can Animate'. They had been creating a short animation using objects to hand such as a Duplo brick and some wild animals. The children from the 'Light and Dark' Learning Group observed this and became so excited about it that they wanted to make an animation about what they had learned.

Recognising this, the educators from the Learning Group consulted the children about how they could relate this to what they had been learning about light and dark. The children became excited about the possibility of making a film, they then took on the idea of animals and creating a place where animals lived and came up with a storyline about animals, 'Honeyland', restricting it to the sub-group theme of hibernating animals, which was the most recent piece of research for some of the children.

It was at this point that the educators needed to consider their roles in and with the Learning Group. Should they follow the sub-group children's interest in animals and 'Honeyland', or should they help the children to focus on their initial overall interest and use their enthusiasm for animation to further this learning? Or had the Learning Group completed its wider role in supporting the children's interest in light and dark?

The head of nursery and one of the adult educators in the Learning Group, decided that perhaps this was a good opportunity to reflect with the children on what they had been learning about and to 'check out' with the group what was to happen next. They shared what they had learned so far and explored whether making a story about what they had learned about light and dark would continue to interest them. She also explored with the other educators if this software package would be a powerful provocation for further learning.

They decided that the response from the children would help them to come to a decision on where they would go next with their interest and their research into it. When the children were reminded about their light and dark research, their focus and enthusiasm about shadows came through strongly. The group agreed that they would make a story about shadows. This launched this group into other avenues of learning. A 'storyboard' format was used to support the children in their understanding of how to write a story. This included learning about the importance of sequential events, choosing characters, designing the characters, how to use ICT to write the story, plot lines and how to use the 'I Can Animate' software, in which they had taken such an interest.

Writing the story

Once the concept for the story was in place the group decided that they wanted to produce a book illustrating the story. They started to design characters for the book. They worked together to create the characters and then decided as a group which characters should go into the book. The children chose princesses, giants and policemen as their main characters. These characters, though unrelated to light and dark, were side interests along the way that some of the children in the Learning Group developed in other areas of the nursery. For example, one of the girls, called Honey, was interested in princesses within home area play and one of the children, Alexander, was keenly interested in policeman, whilst the giant had been an ongoing interest in the nursery over a long period of time. Importantly, the educators in the Learning Group decided to absorb them into the topic and the story. The initial theme for the book was 'why the princess's shadow had disappeared', but this changed as the story gained its own momentum and another title emerged that reflected more accurately the content of the eventual story.

The animation

It is important to remember here that the 'I Can Animate' software was the initial provocation that led the Learning Group to decide they wanted to write a story they could animate. There was intense activity around 'getting into the skin' of the story, which included the children becoming engaged in a lot of role-play experiences related to princesses, policeman and giants. Once this process had been exhausted the 'Light and Dark' Learning Group were ready to start preparing for the animation and invite other interested children to help them.

Creating the sets

Meeting the characters

Image of owl

Marcus dance and photo editing,
Croftamie Nursery

Ways of seeing

Above and overleaf: Maya original painting and 3 colour variations, Croftamie Nursery

Children's planning

Children's gallery

Children painting at the waterfall

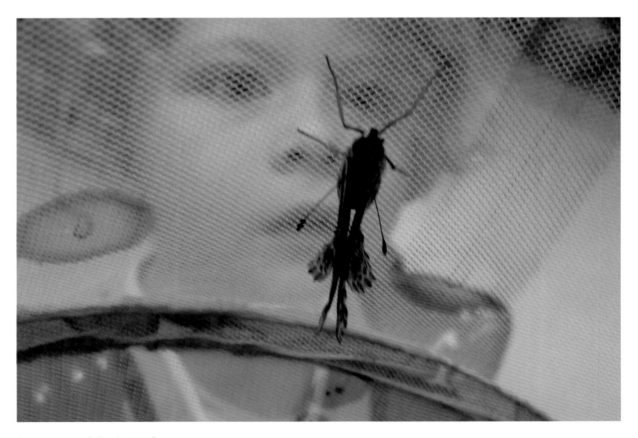

Emergence of the butterfly

Important factors about the animation process:

- The children decided on making the main characters from the story the princess, giant and policemen. These were made from plasticine. A connection was recognised to previous model making where children had learned that they needed a wire skeleton to support the movement of the model. (One educator had also been doing research and watched a film about the making of a Wallace and Gromit film, which was helpful to share in their collaboration process with the children in their preparation for their animation.)
- Sets needed to be made: this included the princess's bedroom and the town where the giant lived. The educator had to work out how many stills needed to be taken so that when a sequence was run it didn't go too fast or too slow. This was important work to be done first so that children understood what they were to do and that they didn't lose interest by all of this being worked out with them. The children were required to take seven stills of the model before moving it slightly and taking another until the sequence had been completed to allow the character to stand up or get out of bed. What was very important was the video camera had to be taped down so it couldn't be knocked and the children were very careful not to knock over any of the models in a very confined space, i.e. the set (see plate section).

The enthusiasm and interest in creating a story began to spread. The excitement, joy and energy from the children and adults involved in this learning collaboration was contagious and 'infected' the rest of the nursery.

> Nothing without Joy!
>
> *L. Malaguzzi cited in Rinaldi 2013, 12*

As the story evolved the educators increasingly understood that the children were making connections between their prior learning and their current learning. This became apparent throughout the story as characters were chosen and designed by children, e.g. policemen, princesses and giants.

For example, when writing about why the princess's shadow had disappeared the children drew upon their experience of 'shadows are made by the blocking of light'. The children wanted the shadow to be revealed by the giant blowing a cloud away, which was blocking the sun. This was reflected also in the eventual title for the story 'Fee, Fi, Fo, Fum: I Haven't Taken the Sun'.

As well as developing the actual content of the story the Learning Group began to explore how to create a Word version of their story book. The children learned how to scan their designs, copy and paste into the Word document. The educators had also been learning about software that could download and turn a Word document into a published book format. The technology skills that the children developed were considerable and they all delighted in how it was able to animate their story as well as resulting ultimately into a published book.

The children in the Learning Group were so excited when they realised that they could have their book 'published'. One of the many thrills from the publication of this book was of course that they could now be referred to as authors. Copies of the book were made and some were given to the library in the local community as well as the mobile library bus, thereby making it available to a wider child audience. Families also purchased copies, which

The Learning Group: writing our story

made the children feel very proud of their work. This remains as a powerful and concrete memory for these children, not only of their project but also of their friends in the setting. This will be a touchstone for them, of an early years experience that helped them to understand the joy and fun of learning. For the early years setting it remains as a permanent reminder of these children but also is an important reference point to their own learning.

What happened next?

Once the children had published the story there were moments throughout the day where children were observed retelling the story to others and beginning to act the story out in the home area. The educators discussed and agreed that they should try to provoke further learning in this area by adding giant's clothes to the house corner for the children to discover and to see where this learning would go. On discovering the clothes the children were amazed at the size and wondered who they belonged to. The children started to compare the size of the clothes with their own bodies and were given time to role-play what being a giant may be like.

Some children had a question they were puzzling with: 'How big is a giant?' The children were given large pieces of paper, which they started to join together and kept asking, 'Is that big enough for a giant?' They kept adding to this until they were satisfied that they had joined enough paper together to represent the height. The question had not yet been answered so then it was decided to measure the giant. The question was then asked: 'How could this be done?' The children decided to use the bricks that were in the area. They gathered the bricks and started to place them in a line from the bottom of the paper to the top and counted how many bricks it would take to make a giant.

Educators seeing the learning that had emerged from the giant's clothes decided to add princess and police costumes as a further provocation. On reflection, it was really at this point that we felt the depth and breadth of the learning that had taken place in the Learning Group; we began to notice the extent to which the learning had travelled. It was not restricted to the 'Light and Dark' Learning Group or to the educators within it; it had spread like a contagion throughout the nursery to the point that everybody was buzzing with the happenings that emerged from this project.

Concluding reflections

What has been very difficult to capture in this chapter is the very nature of how events happened and when. It is important for the reader to understand the complexities of how all educators became involved. Educators were working with different children, sometimes spontaneously and at other times planned. All the educators in the team, at some point, were taking forward different aspects of the project, such as the animation which was running in parallel with the researching of shadows, giants, an owl interest, seasons and hibernation to name but a few. However, what we hope will be obvious is how we were all embracing opportunities to work with this project whenever the opportunity arose, but not to the exclusion of other children who were not involved in it. This is part of the complexity of working in this way, but the learning that emerged from working with this project, for all staff – experienced and new – felt at times seismic, and almost impossible to comprehend. Staff sometimes surprised themselves about the ideas that occurred to them to give this project another dimension and were taken aback when events occurred that were not

Our story is born

Fee! Fi! Fo! Fum!

looked for but appeared at just the right moment to coincide with a particular juncture in the project's development. This project catapulted the staff's understanding about pedagogical documentation and its ability to empower young children to a new level which will be carried forward into future work with young children.

> Thought is the consequence of the provocation of an encounter, with the rhizome of thought shooting in all directions, without beginning or end, but always in between.
>
> *Dahlberg and Moss 2005, 117*

However, what we hope we have communicated in this encounter with pedagogical documentation is that there is much evidence of the children's joy in learning and the way in which they are quite capable of having a voice in what interests them to learn next. This was the key to their sustained engagement here over a period of a year. It also bears witness to the courage of new staff members to 'give it a go' when, as was stated at the beginning, some of them were new to this way of working with young children and had come from early years settings where they were expected to work in very traditional and restrictive ways with young children. What joined them all together, after a hesitant start, was not only the professional dialogue but also the enthusiasm of the children, which caught the imagination of all staff members and infected the whole nursery to the extent that everybody was

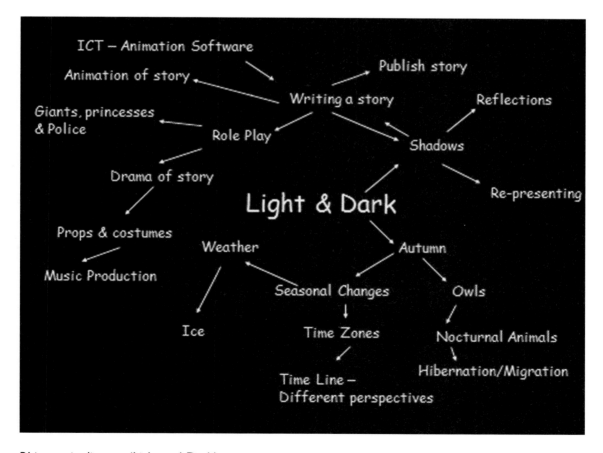

Rhizomatic diagram: 'Light and Dark'

compelled to join in and take the risk that you could make a mistake but quickly recognising that when you do, there will be a view of this that 'we learn by our mistakes', which can be very reassuring to the people coming in new to the documentation approach to learning. The underpinning philosophy that drove this project was a set of values that respected children and adults, had the image of a child as capable, rich and resourceful and gave all those involved, both adults and children, a voice in its ongoing development.

Note

1   The 'Light and Dark' project has been used on many occasions during professional development courses in Stirling and beyond to enlighten, inspire and enthuse members of the audience about pedagogical documentation. It is always our hope that it will prove to them the enormous capacity that young children have to not only learn but to drive their own learning given the opportunity to do so.

Chapter 4

Change as an opportunity

Jackie Dupont and Wendie Garnett

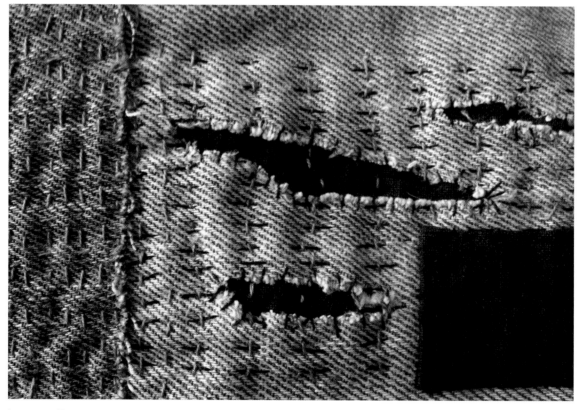

Japanese Boro

Throughout this chapter we look at how the influence of Reggio Emilia, through the implementation of the pedagogical documentation approach to learning, has been the dynamic that has changed the role of the nursery teacher in Stirling Council. We will consider

- why and how it has been remodelled and how the reimagined role sits within other changes in pedagogical practice;

- how the change process has revealed that positive experiences can emerge at times of discontinuity and change;
- how we have understood through our own change process that children can have positive learning experiences while also engaged in situations of discontinuity and change;
- why and how it has been remodelled and how the reimagined role sits within other changes in pedagogical practice.

In 2001, influenced by Reggio Emilia thinking and practice, it was decided to adopt a pedagogical documentation approach to learning within Stirling Council early years settings. Whilst initially this applied to only five nurseries, as it developed into a whole Council approach to early learning it became clear that a more in-depth model of supporting staff was needed than was currently in place. At that time some nurseries had a full-time nursery teacher whose role could be as much administrative as it was supportive of best practice. What was increasingly understood was that for pedagogical documentation to become embedded into practice a more dedicated practice role needed to be found for the nursery teachers. With this in mind the nursery teacher role was remodelled as part of Stirling's pedagogical vision to one that took its inspiration from that of the pedagogista role in Reggio Emilia, which had proved to be very successful in supporting best early years thinking and practice there. To adopt a model similar to this was, therefore, considered to be a good fit to facilitate and sustain a documentation approach to early learning in Stirling Council, not only in the respective settings but also at times to support it through different models of professional development encounters.

In Stirling the pedagogista model, though reflecting the Reggio Emilia pedagogista role, is a hybrid of it. In Reggio Emilia the pedagogistas are based centrally and whilst their core remit, as in Stirling, is to support the development of pedagogical documentation in early years settings, how they achieve this is different. The Reggio Emilia role encompasses a range of roles including professional development both locally and internationally, supporting settings in developing best practice and projects and being responsible for the documentation and resource base in Reggio Emilia etc.

Taking the Stirling model forward meant that a group of fourteen teachers formed the original pedagogista team in August 2007, working with three nurseries each; due to budget cuts, this number was reduced in 2011 to 7 teachers working with six early years settings. The group was, and continues to be, supported by professional training and by collegiate meetings that develop a sense of shared meaning, understandings and purpose. At its inception it was an exciting time, one of innovation and expectation for the pedagogistas embarking on this new role. Initially they were caught, both by their own habits and the expectations of others, between old and new roles. They quickly realised that they were confronted with a tussle; with a 'change process' that affected not just them but also the staff teams, children and families they were working alongside. They tried to juggle both roles in a thirteen-week time span as they felt their way in the dark. Their 'torch' was the awareness that their first step would always be the building of relationships with staff, children and families. A big issue for them was the title! Whilst it was part of the Stirling Council vision to use either the title 'pedagogista' or 'pedagogue', it was quickly realised that neither of these were titles to which staff and families could easily relate. To this day neither of these titles is used widely, but for the purpose of being true to the Stirling Council vision and looking to the future, throughout this chapter we will refer to them as pedagogistas.

How the change process has revealed that positive experiences can emerge at times of change and discontinuity

> It's not so much that we are afraid of change or so in love with the old ways, but it's that place in between that we fear … it's like being between trapezes. It's Linus when his blanket is in the dryer, there is nothing to hold on to.
>
> *Marilyn Ferguson, American Futurist, cited in Bridges 2011, 3*

Whilst there was an enthusiasm among the pedagogistas and service leaders to implement this change of role, there was a confusion about it and the part it was intended to play in embedding pedagogical documentation into usual practice. It has been speculated that the initial timing of the role change may have been untimely, however, what is well known is that there may never be a right time for change and it is only in the living of it that we understand a new situation and come to see its benefits as well as the possible negatives around the initial change process itself. In some ways the role was being constructed as it was lived. Looking back, the core remit of facilitating the documentation approach and supporting its sustainability by offering an additional external viewpoint to pedagogical discourse and links across settings was perhaps understated. It has also been a reflection of the fact that when major changes are made within an already changing culture, time and a certain amount of challenge and pain are required to grow the new concept until transitions are made and staff able to relate to new role identities.

> It isn't the changes that do you in, it's the transitions.
>
> *Ibid.*

Time, personal experience and professional discourse were needed to give the opportunity for people to ask and explore: 'What does the role mean and how can it best serve the envisioned pedagogy?"

The role has had to embrace changes such as the shortening of the blocks of time allocated to each setting, but a naturally occurring increase in ease and flexibility of movement between settings has led directly to a change in our thinking of how we are using pedagogical documentation to 'weave' the gaps between contexts and to support ourselves, staff, children and families in making visible the processes of learning that are being developed by children as they take, adapt and apply their learning from one place to another.

> The relationship between teacher and child is worked out by bringing into relationship their respective strategic contributions within the interaction, not with the view of making different points of view homogenous and consistent, but in order to understand how different points of view are constructed reciprocally. The teacher's role is identified as the main 'connector' of elements, points of view, and relationships within an educational context that, while not accommodating randomness of thoughts and actions, is nonetheless capable of being open to the unpredictable and to chance.
>
> *Fortunati 2006, 75*

Over time, the relationship between pedagogistas, educators, deputes and heads has developed and strengthened to a more reciprocal understanding of the other's role. A major challenge for the pedagogistas was how to manage a greater degree of flexibility of movement between settings, ensuring that over a year there would be an equality of pedagogista input.

> It's not a problem because I know if a situation arises when we feel we would like you to join us from another setting this could happen.
>
> *Educator, early years setting*

This is now a common response from both educators and management teams; time can have the ability to bring sense to change, in the action to integrate it, to formulate certain schemas of action 'on the spot', and to enable oneself to gather the maximum certainty for confronting that which is uncertain.

In these early days an important part of the role of the pedagogista was holding an emotional space in which relationships could be grown and foundations established, as groups of individuals became teams. With a strong foundation the uncertainties offered by the future could be faced and embraced together. There is a growing understanding that the pedagogista must give time to learn about and accommodate variations in the culture and ethos of each setting, informed by geography, history and the uniqueness of each setting. The role begins then with listening – really listening – to both the adults, who support the children through their learning and understanding, and to the children themselves, always being open to making changes and adapting to the needs of the children and educators within the respective settings. Together, pedagogistas and educators negotiate a place where a professional dialogue can begin and select and weave threads together in partnership, developing and strengthening the acts of making visible children's learning within a documentation approach to early learning.

In addition, through dialogue with the teams that the pedagogistas work alongside, the value of the threads or traces they leave behind for children and adults has been recognised. These can be visible across a range of media or reflections, attitudes and approaches, which slowly emerge and reveal the positive impact of the pedagogista's influence in the respective settings They have come to understand that these threads may not be picked up immediately and that patience and persistence are key to their role in bringing about change. Another valuable part of the role is to continue collecting – from their own experience, reading, discourse, other settings and reflection etc. – and offering threads of ideas, whilst unsure who will pick them up or when, or how they will combine them or reimagine them; always hoping that at some point they will be encountered and become catalysts for new thinking, and new ways of working. Pedagogistas can be surprised at times at how staff and children pick these threads up and weave them into their own unique patterns, often after they have moved on. It has come to be recognised that this is part of the complex, multi-layered nature of the pedagogista role and of the documentation approach. Significantly, it has been one of the many challenges of working within this role and system for pedagogistas to readily let go of their own enthusiasms and ideas and see themselves as catalysts for others on their roads to developing deeper understandings of pedagogical documentation.

How pedagogistas have increasingly understood through their own change process that there are situations where children and staff teams can develop positive learning connections while also engaged in situations of change and discontinuity

As mentioned earlier it is not just early years pedagogista roles that have been changing; the staff teams they work with have been managing their own change challenges. In some cases, alongside adjusting to the discontinuation of the full-time teacher model and adapting to the pedagogista model, they were being asked to implement a documentation approach to early learning. For some staff teams this paradigm shift was causing both anxiety and uncertainty about how to develop this with the children and also enter into conversations with parents about its values and importance in revealing young children as capable and competent people. The discontinuation of the teacher role and the discontinuity of the pedagogista model raised different questions for the educators and the families. The key to accommodating both these elements of change lay in the way the pedagogistas approached their role with educators, families and management teams. Once it became clear that their main function was to support staff in developing a best practice approach to pedagogical documentation, pathways to learning together began to open up.

Elaine, one of the educators in Aberfoyle Nursery shared that the opportunity to engage in the documentation approach to learning with the support of the pedagogista has changed her life.

> I just love it, I love the way the children grow when given trust and opportunities to work things out themselves. When they revisit documentation and explain it to the young ones the children are consolidating their own learning in their own heads and deepening their own understandings – in some cases you can see new levels of understanding dawn on them that maybe weren't there before. The children who have been in nursery and have become familiar with this way of working see themselves as the 'experts' while others join in on the journey and gain their own expertise. I think my own understanding of documentation, of the value in making learning visible keeps taking another leap forward – the more I look and share with others, and that sharing is so important, the more light bulbs go on and I can see deeper. It's so exciting.

Change in another sense became an opportunity when children who had moved from the same nursery into the primary school setting reflected back after two years onto their time there on a space project they had been involved in to resource their building of a rocket. Together with their new teacher they revisited their previous project and this learning they applied to a different, though related, topic. Change of context did not dim the ability of these children to use learning from a previous situation and apply it to a another topic.

Staff changing from one setting to another can also be seen as an opportunity to influence positively ways of working in the new setting; threads of previous experiences being woven, tentatively at first, into the fabric of the receiving setting. A good example of this was when an educator who moved within Stirling Council from a small rural establishment to a large urban nursery. The educator saw his change of context as an opportunity to introduce a different visibility of documentation to those currently being used in his new nursery and which he had used and developed in his previous setting. These were A4 books to record individual children's learning and this change of visibility has meant that children and families were able to access them more freely than ring binders and PowerPoint presentations, which were the preferred options of the new setting. Families, as well as children, have benefited from this change of visibility, which has also been extended to make visible ongoing projects in the setting. One change has spawned another. The educator and the pedagogista took responsibility for this change of practice and the educator has reflected that

> Each child starts with the same blank book, as they leave their traces each child makes it their own, impressing their personality on the pages. The books have deepened our understanding as a team. They make learning clearer, they show detail of progression and depth of learning. Importantly they encourage families to want to know and find out more about their children's learning … about the progression.

Interestingly, for reasons not yet clearly discerned, this change of visibility has been very popular with parents and families since they have been much keener to contribute to them than any other previous visibility used by this early years setting.

This particular change would be an understanding that the pedagogista would use to influence the practice of other settings into which he/she moved, taking into account that what might work in one setting would not necessarily have the same impact on another. The importance of these connecting threads cannot be underestimated in influencing the whole of the change process within the Stirling Council settings.

By knowing the staff, children and families that the pedagogistas work with the potential can be seen to draw these ends of threads together and sharing the opportunities to weave them together in new and reimagined ways.

How it can be understood through the pedagogista's own change process that children can have positive learning experiences while also engaged in situations of discontinuity and change

Changing from working in three settings to six has enabled a different and personal way for the pedagogista to experience discontinuity of learning and to find/seek the benefits of moving between different environments. By embracing the discontinuities and advantage of feeling settled within a context, settling in and the anticipation of an impending change can provide an impetus for both pedagogistas and educators. Children can likewise be faced with similar changing environments not only between home and one nursery but sometimes between home and two nursery settings; this being to accommodate the working patterns of their families. This kind of situation that children find themselves in can often be seen as detrimental to the child, as indeed it can be depending on their disposition and background. But it has been a recent understanding of the pedagogistas that this movement between settings can have beneficial outcomes for the child as it does for them; particularly so if the pedagogista and the child/children are moving between the same two settings. A child moving between two settings will see in the pedagogista a familiar adult who is also moving between the same two settings; a perfect opportunity to support transference and consolidation of learning and understanding between two different learning environments.

As Aldo Fortunati suggests

> In short, one could attempt to redefine the problem of separation in new terms, as a path shared by the child and the family in which each subject experiments with his or her own attachments, limits and possibilities in situations in which they are together or separated.
>
> On one hand this requires that the family view the child not so much in terms of him being subject to the necessity of a choice made by others – 'I have to send him to the infant-toddler centre' – but instead crediting the child with abilities and giving value to the fact that he is capable of being actively engaged in the situations he confronts, in particular those which involve him together with peers outside the protective realm of family figures.
>
> *Fortunati 2006, 45*

In this instance Fortunati is talking about the child settling in to one establishment with confidence and both child and parent embracing this as a positive learning/life experience. What really struck a chord was the echo heard from many parents about feeling guilt: 'I have to send him to the infant-toddler centre.' The last few years of working within and between settings has provided opportunities for pedagogistas to explore some of the dominant issues around the dis/continuity of learning that occurs when children move from one setting to another. What has been somewhat of an insight for them is the way some children are able to manage and indeed benefit from moving between different settings within their daily and weekly routines.

Ross

Ross is a child (4 years old) who has a 'split' placement. This means he moves between two settings; a nursery session within a local authority primary school two days a week and a full day placement at a 'partnership' nursery for three days per week. This arrangement coincided with one of the pedagogistas covering the same two settings. Arising from this situation, positive opportunities and connections through change for the child that had not been apparent before to the pedagogista came into focus. A much deeper understanding of what is meant by 'working in the gap' and 'seeing the threads of dispositions to learning' was made evident through pedagogical documentation. What happened here was because both the child and the pedagogista were moving between the same two settings, new and different connections were able to be made and built upon. Without the documentation moving between the settings with both the child and the pedagogista, it may not have been possible either to make these connections or to understand what they could mean.

The connecting thread between both settings

The attention of the pedagogista was caught when Ross made, at the local authority nursery, a 'polar bear' with the inclusion of a thought bubble. The pedagogista knew that thought bubbles had been introduced at Ross's partnership nursery, where she was for a period of time, when the children visited the author Oliver Jeffers live video site (the site was visited as part of the children's interest in Oliver Jeffers' story 'Lost and Found' and their interpretation of this story through making and using 'stick' puppets as 'props' to retell the story). Ross's understanding of the purpose of thought bubbles was further consolidated a few days later when there was a change in interest from animals to numbers and how to keep safe in the local environment. He used his understanding and knowledge of thought bubbles to enhance his own input into the planning process and make clear what he would like to learn about next.

Ross: I'm thinking about traffic lights and what colours they should be.

At this point other children in the nursery were also interested in how Ross was showing his thoughts:

Innes: I'm going to draw a huey [a very simple line drawing of a person, with a thought bubble, favoured by Oliver Jeffers] as well and he's going to be thinking about counting to 100.

On returning to the local authority nursery Ross, with a group of children and an adult, was revisiting the values of the nursery. After some discussion the children were asked to draw or to represent their ideas of what was important for them when they were at nursery and how they and their friends and adults should behave when at nursery. Ross drew a huey with a thought bubble and another child picked up on the idea and developed it in his own

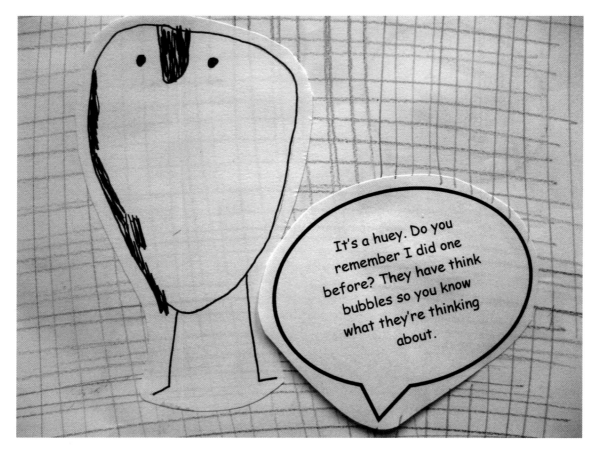

The speech bubbles (used in the Huey)

Above and overleaf: The Huey (children's adaptation)

representation. Since the pedagogista was present at this setting also, it meant that she understood that Ross was transferring his learning from one nursery to another, thus causing her to consider the positives that can derive from a child changing from one context to another.

This example illustrates how the movement of both pedagogistas and children between settings can allow connections to be made between shared learning experiences but also deepens understanding of it and can also initiate friendships. It is the act of documentation, the revisiting of this documentation and the sharing of it with the child (as the initiator), all educators at each setting and the parents, that enabled Ross to develop a sense of control and purpose as he moves between contexts.

Alex and Callum

In a rural nursery in Stirling another example of viewing discontinuity in a positive sense revealed itself again, this time in a different form. Here two children, Alex and Callum, were working together on model making. The two had previously been active participants in an exploration of sticking and fixing materials and had started making a vehicle together with boxes. Their attendance patterns, however, often did not coincide, so without any formal agreement they both worked on the model separately. Each would come in and check out what his friend had added, commenting on a change in perceived function or shape or a particularly interesting and successful addition or technique before contributing his own contribution to the model. Neither child complained or made criticism of the other, just 'I wonder what he was thinking there?' or 'Hmmm, he seems to be turning it into...' This collaboration was enabled by the value educators placed on the shared construction process and the actual model, always finding somewhere for it to dry safely and giving time and importance to the role of being witness to both the process and work without overt 'interference'.

This example shows the ability of children to rise above the possible distractions that discontinuity of patterns of attendance and friendships can bring, provided that the process with which they are engaging is understood and supported by pedagogistas, educators and families.

Conclusion

How these children responded to these changed situations they were in, caused the pedagogistas to be thoughtful about their own coping mechanisms through continual movement and adjustment between settings, adapting to new routines and getting to understand new sets of colleagues. Ross's tool for connecting the threads was a simple representation that not only consolidated a piece of learning for him but also appealed to other children who adopted it. This led to important connections with other children, which helped Ross to form new friendships in the local authority nursery. Callum and Alex used their model as a tool to make connections with each other, discontinuity of attendance not being an obstacle.

The pedagogista's tool for connecting the threads is making relationships with families, listening to the children and engaging in professional dialogue with the educators. What the two authors of this chapter see as a metaphor for weaving these particular threads together is the Japanese Bora, where different patches of threads are woven in at various times in much the same way as their role can be depending on the ebb and flow of the respective settings where they find themselves. Like the pedagogista's role, the Boro is never finished and can always be added to or unpicked and reworked to produce another pattern or richness.

Chapter 5

Powerful Images, Visible Learning

Brian Hartley

'Powerful Images, Visible Learning' developed out of a desire to improve the quality of photography taken by staff at nursery establishments in Stirling, by working with an experienced artist who had an understanding of working with children, who could support and inspire staff and children. There was an established practice within the nursery settings to use cameras to document children's learning, and a firm belief in the importance of photography to support and enable effective learning. Digital cameras were becoming more and more effective as a tool within the nursery thanks to rapidly changing technology and much more accessible, user-friendly and affordable cameras that could enhance the learning experience for both staff and children. Although digital cameras had been used in nursery settings for many years there was a desire to utilise cameras more effectively as part of the documentation approach and also upgrade the camera provision from the existing resources to more advanced and better quality equipment that could capture high quality images more effectively.

The Artist

I am a visual artist and designer based in Glasgow, and I have a multi-disciplinary career in the arts. I studied at Glasgow School of Art and I have worked extensively with arts education projects for many years. I first worked in Stirling in 2007 as part of a design project entitled 'The Six Cities Design Festival', a national design festival that took place simultaneously in Scotland's six cities: Aberdeen, Dundee, Edinburgh, Glasgow, Inverness and Stirling.

The provocation

Baker Street Nursery in Stirling hosted a project led by The Lighthouse, Scotland's centre for design and architecture, with a team of designers working across a range of disciplines from sound design to interior design, with me bringing experience in stage design and visual art and experience in working with young children. Using an action research methodology the project investigated ways to enable the children to follow their creative interests and ideas, and to bring the artistic team's designs skills into a dialogue to realise these ideas. The project developed over a three-month period and explored innovative ways to re-imagine the creative spaces in the nursery. Throughout this creative process the nursery staff were involved and active in recording and capturing the children's responses, which were then revisited with the children and the designers.

Following the success of this project I was invited to bring more of my skills and knowledge to the education services in Stirling, to present a visual arts masterclass at a creativity conference in the autumn of 2007, and share some of my experiences when working at Baker Street Nursery. Arising from both these involvements I was invited to work more extensively with the nurseries/schools in Stirling on a project which became known as 'Powerful Images, Visible Learning' the emphasis of which initially was to be around supporting staff teams and children to develop their expertise in photography.

Visible learning, powerful images

> Documentation ... is seen as visible listening, as a construction of traces (through notes, slides, videos and so on) that not only testify to the children's learning processes, but also make them possible because they are visible, for us this means making visible, and thus possible, the relationships that are the building blocks of knowledge.
>
> *Rinaldi 2006, 68*

Designing a project

To initiate this project a group of nursery heads formed a Learning Group as a way to work together and develop a deeper understanding of a documentation approach to early learning, with a commitment to identifying, understanding, analysing, supporting and sharing children's learning. The need for specialist support in photography was a key aim of this research and I was approached by a Senior Link Officer in Stirling to bring my skills in photography and experience of working with young children to this ongoing dialogue, and to work very closely with experienced staff and children at Stirling Council. Over the course of the research, the group developed some key aims, objectives, intentions and a methodology to take forward this work in practical terms with a small group of nursery settings who would participate in a practical research project working with me. The work would evolve in collaboration with myself, staff teams, children and the specific context of each setting. These key aims and objectives were:

- assist staff in choosing and the purchase of new resources;
- enable staff teams to make the best use of the resources at their disposal;
- enhance images taken of children, by working alongside staff on technique;
- develop staff understanding of production and post-production of images;
- develop staff understanding of how to capture learning through effective use of digital cameras;
- build on staff understanding of how children learn and the power of making this visible in a variety of ways.

In order to take this forward I worked with staff using a variety of methods (set out in the Interim Report), including:

- an audit of equipment, which was to be needs-based in the respective settings;
- work alongside staff and children on the nursery floor, and also with key staff on more specific one-to-one workshop sessions;
- staff team discussion and planning;
- production of a PowerPoint presentation to share the processes and outcomes of the work.

In using cameras as a vital part of the process of documentation of children's learning we reflected on the work of Alison Clark and Peter Moss in their book *The Mosaic Approach to Learning*.

> Cameras offer young children the opportunity to produce a finished product in which they can take pride. Children who have seen members of their family take photographs, poured over family albums or looked at photographs in books and comics, know that photographs have a value in the 'adult world'. This is always the case with children's own drawings and paintings. Photographs offer a powerful new language for young children. It is a language that children can use to convey their feelings as well as information through the 'silent voice of the camera'.
>
> *Clark and Moss 2001, 28*

The project

The initial phase of the 'Powerful Images, Visible Learning' project began with five settings and the work spanned two staff training days in the academic year, with shared learning opportunities for the group at the beginning and end of the process. Through the consultation process there was a genuine willingness to learn and explore the camera and photography, combined with an in-depth experience of children's learning and a desire to support the development of staff confidence and creative skills.

At the beginning of the project all the participating staff teams met as a group to take part in a session where the project was introduced through a presentation, followed by group discussions and workshop activities. The session was led by the Senior Link Officer and I gave a PowerPoint presentation featuring background information about photography and digital cameras, examples of compositional techniques and powerful images from the history of photography as a provocation and inspiration to staff. Following this there was a discussion about the project aims and intentions, staff teams discussed hopes and expectations, and there was a practical workshop session to explore practical ways to evaluate composition.

The aims and objectives of the project, and key learning outcomes and questions devised by the learning group provided a clear framework to engage with each nursery setting, and by developing the practical work over several visits and a sustained period of time allowed a deeper engagement and opportunities for reflection and revisiting learning.

The project provided a new digital camera for each setting. I provided advice on the choice of camera based on: an assessment of several key technical features, price range, that they were robust enough for children to use as well as adults, and that they supported the aspirations of the project.

I visited each setting several times over the course of the project, beginning with an initial consultation with educators to identify key hopes, expectations and specific questions. This was followed by several creative and practical workshop sessions with staff and children, so that I could get to know the nursery and work with as many children and educators as possible. Staff and children were encouraged to use the camera as much as possible during the project and of course this added many more photographs to be reviewed and stored, but it also required a more rigorous editing and selection process and opportunity for learning. The work evolved and was tailored to each setting and their specific needs and stages of development, recognising a wide range of experience and confidence amongst staff. At various times it ranged from intensive one-to-one tuition in basic camera use, to group learning with staff or practical work on the nursery floor with the children using cameras.

At the end of the process there was a further group meeting with all of the participating settings, with each setting invited to present key outcomes and reflections on the work, sharing key moments within their creative journey, specific learning, and reflecting the diversity of ways that the cameras had been used. Within this event I revisited the introductory PowerPoint presentation, allowing a further opportunity to assess learning and reflect on new knowledge and experience gained during the project. This event proved to be a very positive and inspiring session. It provided an opportunity for sharing ideas, further learning and reflection amongst the staff teams, seeing different approaches and ways of thinking. There was also an opportunity for more in-depth conversation around the learning involved and a discussion about where and how to further develop and continue the work. It had a tangible benefit on efficiency and productivity amongst staff and in many cases created a stronger team with skills being shared, and mutual support enabling every member of the staff team to feel valued and learn effectively at their own level.

After the conclusion of the nursery presentations it was evident that the work had developed in diverse ways in each setting, reflecting the multiple perspectives, skills and values of the staff teams and children.

In the light of such a positive and lasting impact from the pilot project the settings were committed to sustaining and further developing the work, and sharing what they had learned with others.

The Interim Report recorded the feedback from the staff teams after completing the process which was very positive.

> An exciting atmosphere was created in the nursery, all sorts of potential and possibilities were sparked off.

> Empowerment of educators and staff by having a boost/kick-start through the involvement of an expert.

> Sharing of documentation – children taking images of what interested them, educators supporting children to learn how to process their images, put them onto the computer, print them out.

Children finding out by chance, but then 'using the chance, remembering it and using it again very quickly'.

The results and positive feedback from the five participating settings created a demand from the wider nursery settings across the Council area to take part in the project. Proposals were developed to secure additional funding to deliver it in further groups of settings from stand-alone nursery settings to nurseries within schools reflecting the diversity of early years provision in Stirling Council. The intention now was that by the completion of the project in 2013, I would have worked with thirty settings spread across six separate groups with an awareness of the underlying vision and principles of the wider Council early years education policy which had pedagogical documentation at its core.

> Seeing comes before words. The child looks and recognises before it can speak... But there is also another sense in which seeing comes before words. It is seeing which establishes our place in the surrounding world; we explain that world with words, but word can never undo the fact that we are surrounded by it. The relation between what we see and what we know is never settled... Soon after we can see, we are aware that we can also be seen. The eye of the other combines with our own eye to make it fully credible that we are part of the visible world.
>
> *Berger 1972, 71*

Some of the following cameos from the nurseries that I worked with heightened my own ways of seeing and required from the educators a specific focus and a way of seeing that was 'out of the box' and open to chance allowing creativity to become more dominant in thinking and practice.

What would Bunny see?

> Brian encouraged us to think about taking images from different points of view, different perspectives, different levels (above, below etc.). Florence saw this and wanted to see what she looked like from her Bunny's point of view. An image was taken of her from his point of view and through conversation around this our combined thinking went out of the box – What would Bunny see if he were lying on a box looking up? The images of this enabled Florence to share Bunny's story with others which provoked further experimentation with the camera.
>
> *Educator at Aberfoyle Nursery*

Working at Aberfoyle Nursery in rural Stirling discussions with a girl about her eye level led to a series of photographs in the nursery looking at furniture from different angles: under the table, over the chair and so on, all considering where the eye level was in each image. These photographs were revisited with the educator and demonstrated the child's and the adult's growing understanding of how the camera could contribute to 'different ways of seeing' (see plate section).

Torches

In another nursery setting the camera was able to respond to children's interests across other curricular areas. The children were actively interested in a space theme that had become firmly established for some time. The staff had created a solar system with large models of the planets constructed with the children, and it was clearly evident that this theme was actively inspiring the children. In thinking how could the camera support this learning it was decided to use the 'night' setting on the camera to take long exposure photos within a small playroom where the lights could be turned off. The educator and the artist gave the children torches and asked them, as photographs were taken, to move the torches at different speeds creating light trails and images that the children thought were like shooting stars. The children then explored the concept of day and night using the torches to shine on a globe and using the camera on a night setting to take photos of how the light falls on one part of the globe at a time. Several groups of children participated in this experience learning from taking photographs themselves, others watching how they were taken. The activity's life was extended by revisiting the session through sharing the images and experiences with other children. The practical aspects of the activity were revisited on another day allowing the children a further opportunity to take more images to deepen the children's understanding of the ideas and themes in the session (see plate section).

> After working with the children on the 'torch' episode the children actually started to use the screen on the camera and notice that some images were better than others … because they could look back and talk about their images immediately looking at the camera screen and also images made larger through connecting to the computer … the children were critical of their own work especially when seen on the big screen, they would pick pictures they weren't pleased with and delete them. The physical movement needed to make the light trails attracted children who would not normally have been interested in camera work. If I hadn't been involved with this work with Brian I don't think I would have become so interested in the workings of the camera which led to working with the children to look at the 'macro' button … and after that to use the 'Stop Motion' programme to make animations with the children … the project provided more interest in cameras for me as well as for the children.
>
> *Educator at Braehead Nursery*

Maya's colours

On a visit to Croftamie I worked with a girl called Maya and an educator. Maya was very interested in painting and had created a colourful painting on canvas. I showed Maya how to take a photograph of the painting and download it onto the computer so that she could see it on the computer screen, initially using the zoom function to look closer at the image in great detail and then zooming out to see the whole image, and then working with some editing software where the colours of the painting could be changed. The educator was interested in observing how Maya would respond to the changes. After looking at several colour variations Maya commented afterwards 'I was making it different colours but not drawing on it, I used the computer, I also learned that I could make my favourite colours light or dark, but afterwards I like my painting the way I painted it.' (see plate section)

This showed a sense that the Maya had the capability to make clear decisions when creating her artwork, and that even the opportunity on screen to see her work in different ways did not alter her original creative choices.

Marcus

In a predominantly female environment the role of a man, particularly with camera expertise, can create another dynamic that can cause children to change their 'way of seeing' as is illustrated in this cameo from one nursery.

Marcus was part of a small group of boys reluctant to join in music and movement with the girls. Through discussions between the children it was decided to incorporate their interest in being active outdoors with photography. Marcus was extremely enthusiastic at the activity and participated energetically creating lots of dramatic movement and many photographs were taken of the sequences of movement capturing the activity in detail. Afterwards Marcus revisited the images on the computer, and was able to relive the experience with the educators. While on the computer, working with myself and the educator, Marcus was able to change the colours in the photograph and to independently change the images, experiencing shading, highlighting features, silhouettes, and change light and dark. This process of editing and transforming the images gave Marcus a different viewpoint of the movement session, commenting 'that's so cool' and afterwards Marcus and the other boys did join in with future movement activities (see plate section).

Transforming my way of seeing

On reflecting on the process with which I had been engaged in Stirling Council early years settings, my background and training as a visual artist, and multi-disciplinary artistic practice presented many opportunities for learning and exploring different ways of seeing in an educational setting. I felt that I could be a creative catalyst and invite staff to experiment with the cameras. My artistic background enabled me to respond creatively and in unexpected ways to what I experienced in the nurseries and my working knowledge of different art mediums and experience creating dance for young children added a further level of experience that many educators were keen to benefit from. My work as a photographer, the necessity to respond quickly to capture moving images was an essential skill in understanding the work required of the educators to record the children's learning. My experience in arts education projects gave a context for understanding children's creativity, however, the breadth of knowledge that I gained during the project was much more specific and in-depth than I had previously encountered in shorter-term projects. The specific methodology in Stirling did require new understandings of ways to listen more carefully and engage in decision making with young children. The depth of attention that staff paid to the children and ways that they all learn together I found very different to previous creative projects. Working so closely in an educational context inspired me to learn more about childhood development, which has informed other aspects of my work. The duration of the work in Stirling allowed a sustained opportunity to learn and research and this time enabled me to become more invested in the connections between creativity and education. I felt that my role as a visiting artist was valued by the nurseries; they understood the role and input that an artist could bring to a nursery context. From learning more about the work of the atelier and the atelierista in the Reggio Emilia methodology I developed a better understanding of how the creative role of an artist as a catalyst and creative expert can complement the pedagogical and educational work of the educators, creating an environment where everyone is able to learn and share ideas together. I understood the value in being in a place where creativity is valued as part of a wider culture of learning and knowledge.

> During Brian's visits to the playrooms and working with the children the nursery had a real buzz of excitement. In a predominantly female environment having a male working with the children can have a different dynamic. Brian quickly engaged with the children in a manner that meant they felt respected. He listened to them asked them questions and truly valued their opinions. The children gained confidence and recognised themselves as specialists.
>
> *Head of Doune Nursery*

Closing reflections

This project grew far beyond my initial expectations and allowed a unique opportunity to learn about early childhood education, although I had come to the project with experience it challenged me to broaden expectations of children's capabilities through seeing so many wonderful examples of creative thinking and the 'joy of learning' and to see so much tangible evidence of how the arts can be an intrinsic part of our development, at a time when the arts seem to be getting squeezed in mainstream education in favour of more academic subjects. To see creativity and learning genuinely valued and supported, and the resulting growth in confidence and skills amongst staff and children and the growth in community and awareness of the environments we live was special. Seeing the project develop across the wider Stirling Council area allowed me to discover many new parts of Scotland and meet many inspired and passionate educators and staff committed to supporting and encouraging children's learning.

Chapter 6

Making learning visible through the use of new technologies

Sharon Milne and Wendie Garnett

Introduction

One of the tenets of the concept of 'making learning visible' is that visual images entice children and families. In homes and nurseries, conversations are frequently enhanced with a picture of a child's latest milestone or a cherished holiday memory. Although the narrator is often an adult, increasingly young children are finding their voice using new technology, as they slide through electronic folders until they find their desired image and wish to share their stories about it. The child has a growing fascination with how easily digital images allow them to look back and reflect, with themselves or others, on a memory or experience. This upsurge and familiarity with electronic media has however brought a note of caution about the increasing amounts of time young children are being exposed to technology (NAEYC and the Fred Rogers Center, 2011). The concern is that their use is a substitute for family interactions and creative play. However, on a positive note, Plowman *et al.* (2011) found children have acquired their technological knowhow from learning situations within their own family. This suggests that technology is an enhancement and not just a substitute for human interaction and creative learning.

In the nursery setting, new technology offers further potential for children, as well as adults, to make visible their own learning and for it to invite more social interaction amongst children, educators and family members. The aim of using these newer technologies is to facilitate conversations about children's enquiry, the extent of their understandings, and the processes, skills and strategies that are being employed in particular learning episodes. This interpretation offers educators insights into ways in which children learn and encourages them to share this with the purpose of deepening the collective learning of the whole community.

Old technology in transformation: 'Powerful Images, Visible Learning' project

In 2008, Brian Hartley, a visual artist, began to work collaboratively with a small group of 'pilot' nurseries within the Stirling Council area. He came to the project as an artist and photographer with previous experience of working within early years. Brian had realised the potential of using photographs creatively to make children's learning visible, and from the start of the project found the dialogue with nursery staff to be similar to the creative conversations he has with artists. In particular, the analysis of various images with an eye for meaning, which ensures their own perspective is opened to other viewpoints and new ideas (see Chapter 5).

The first small group began to research how taking better photographs would enhance the documentation of children's learning experiences by making their learning more explicit. All six nurseries had been working with the documentation approach to learning for a number of years, and the discourse about children's learning was already well established. This enabled the collaboration to focus on the artistic process to see and capture more effectively the world around them. An important part of the project was having a photographer working alongside staff to develop their confidence with cameras and images, to facilitate the capture of enhanced images of children and to engage teams in dialogue about children's learning.

Sharron, an educator in Stirling, reflected on the benefit of having a photographer working alongside her. She cites the capture of the butterfly image (see figure on page 69), and the child's unexpected look of surprise and awe, as a crucial moment that transformed, irrevocably, her thinking.

> What is most significant for me about this particular image is the intensity of Lauren's expression of wonder as she watches the butterfly emerge. You can almost feel what she is feeling. Without the input from Brian, I don't think it would have occurred to me to try a more creative camera angle, and this special moment may have been lost.
>
> *Sharron, Park Drive Nursery*

The role of photographer in Stirling's early years settings has parallels with the role of the atelieristas in the municipal preschools and infant toddler centres of Reggio Emilia. With their artistic backgrounds, atelieristas work with the teachers to foster children's interest in the world around them, to enhance creative opportunities, to open up new possibilities and to assist in the facilitation of learning projects. Atelieristas are fully involved in the documentation process and in doing so support the professional development of teachers.

Brian, the visual artist, was commissioned by Stirling Council for several reasons. Firs, the advent of the digital camera meant that large quantities of images were being taken, and the quality of what was being archived came into question. Second, technology had become more sophisticated and faster, with small digital cameras now having the potential to be more effective in capturing children's learning. Digital cameras are now capable of taking lots of images, including close-ups, which puts the camera at the centre of what the children are experiencing, taking the viewer right into that moment. Modern cameras are discreet, with fewer distracting flashes, allowing the photographer to move away from posed shots towards capturing an experience in action and enabling children's expressions to be more visible. The aim is to capture a learning moment without losing the flow of enquiry from which possible meanings can be hypothesised and interpreted with the children. It should be remembered that photography with all children and adults must remain ethical, with each person having the opportunity to accept or reject being filmed or photographed.

Emergence of butterfly: Lauren's wonder

Throughout the project, staff gained a growing understanding about framing photographs, multiple perspectives, capturing movement, taking close-ups, using different angles and printing varying sizes of photographs to suit the purpose and place. As educators became more creative, children became used to them getting down on the floor or climbing on a chair to capture an image from a different perspective. Brian comments:

> These different perspectives remind the adults that the world is a more unusual place than we may anticipate, and encourage us to look and to see the world in the eyes of the child.

Initially, there had been some anxiety that this new approach would require more work and add pressure in an already busy workload. In fact this has proved otherwise. To make the project more sustainable, the introduction of complex editing software was avoided, and more basic programmes such as Windows Picture Manager were employed. As staff became more confident with photo editing, such as cropping and enlarging photos to hone in on significant details, time was saved. When the emphasis moved from quantity to quality, fewer images and less memory storage was required. Now five years into the initiative, technology has continued to move forwards, with pen drives and external hard drives making the long-term storage of significant images and PowerPoint presentations possible. A continuing challenge is the cost of printing but Brian has helped with this problem too, demonstrating how black and white images can be enhanced by removing the colour saturation and increasing the tone and contrast. Although a black and white camera setting can be used, this prevents the opportunity to print a coloured version of the photograph in the future.

Visual literacy

Just as a child's black-line drawing may show greater detail, a black and white image allows the viewer to focus on form and line rather than colour. The authors are now more aware that as a black and white image benefits from the contrast, our published documentation has to give space to each image. As adults we are regularly exposed to the design principles of visual literacy when we read magazines and newspapers. However, this does not necessarily translate into automatically understanding how to present documentation in a way that can be more easily 'read' by others. An example of this is by adding a white border to an image, the eye is drawn inwards and is focussed on the image. Simply positioning the most powerful image in the top left quadrant of the page where, in western culture, the eye strikes first, can make a significant difference as to how much attention the reader pays to each element on a page (Wien 2011, 5). Interpretation and meaning is made more possible when text that exists in relationship with an image is placed alongside it, making explicit the context and learning of a particular image. Through engaging in dialogue with Brian and the powerful image project there has been a move away from multi-coloured backgrounds, many small images and too much text. From the process of critical analysis came the realisation that the desire to make all children visible only informed the breadth of an experience rather than the depth of learning. In many ways our role is akin to a journalist, who sets out to distribute information effectively. Before documentation is published, discerning choices must be made about to whom the documentation is most relevant, who the audience will be, which images and narrative the children wish to include and what learning processes are to be made visible.

Opening up new possibilities

One strength of the 'Powerful Images, Powerful Learning' project has been the way that educators and photographer have collaborated together to extend and provoke the children's current interests, which have varied from setting to setting. Sharing experiences has been at the core of the project. The retelling of every staff team's learning journey is shared with their particular cohort of six nursery settings at their joint project evaluation. This community of learners benefits from the dialogue with others, which prompts new understandings and raises possibilities for the future. From this perspective, nursery teachers have had a significant role in supporting dialogue about the value and meaning of photographs and subsequent narratives, moving thought processes forwards. Their own dialogue with Brian allows them to disseminate to others shared examples. As Rinaldi (2001, 17) comments, the value of documentation is that it isn't confined to a predefined episode of learning. Instead, it has the potential to be shared many times over and in doing so becomes the catalyst for further learning.

In the following example, the educator has come to recognise how an image acts as a provocation. The initial project captured the interest of children, educators and families, but found further, unexpected, significance a year later, when the original project documentation was revisited.

I'm flying an aeroplane

At Newton Primary, the nursery class was using the camera to help the children learn about scale, distance and size. Working alongside the educator, the photographer's guided participation encouraged a group of children to take photographs of a model dinosaur from a variety of angles and eye levels, and to consider different ways of framing the subject. These images provoked questions about how big the dinosaur appeared to be in comparison to the actual size of the model.

In a further example, Dougie, who was three at the time, was building a Duplo aeroplane. After commenting that a pilot flies an aeroplane, he was asked if he would like to be photographed as the pilot flying his plane. The photograph was set up and the printed image drew many comments from family and friends about the illusion of a small child apparently seated on a Duplo aeroplane.

A year later, the photographs were revisited. Dougie wanted to believe he had been flying the plane, but didn't know how he had achieved this.

The educator's new confidence in the children's abilities with the camera allowed her to transfer the photographer role to Bethan, who took a series of photographs in order to solve the problem of how to appropriately imitate the original perspective. As a result, at age four, both children now appear to have a better understanding of proximal and spatial awareness compared to a year ago, and were able to build upon their previous learning to extend their

I'm flying the aeroplane

Reconstructing the aeroplane

experiences. Later, both children acted as publishers, deciding which of Bethan's photographs was closest to the original photograph. This learning was then reviewed with a larger group, allowing more children the opportunity to further their own understanding of perspective and provoking a ripple effect, where learning moves from the originator outwards to embrace others. The two parts to this learning episode demonstrate how the catalytic power of images first prompts Dougie's question, and shows how Dougie and Bethan's involvement changed from being observers to constructors of the re-enactment.

The educator acknowledged that working alongside a photographer enabled her to see the familiar in unfamiliar ways. She also appreciated that 'less is more', understanding that a powerful image with a meaningful caption has the potential to both invite and engage children and families in further dialogue much more than an extensive display of text-free small photographs. The aeroplane photographs were displayed for longer than usual, allowing children to revisit experiences in order to reflect, to question and to engage in deeper thought processes. Some months later, in February 2012, this learning episode became part of a small exhibition in the local library. The aim was to open discussions about the documentation process with the wider community, to make visible children's thinking and their sharing of ideas through photographs and accompanying dialogue, and to demonstrate the capacity of very young children to participate in critical thinking processes. During the preparation and publishing of exhibition materials, significant thought was given to image size, text amount and font size to capture both the interest of the audience and the context of the learning. One viewer left this thought:

> To see the photographs taken by such young children has had a powerful effect on me this morning. They have such a strong sense of capturing 'the moment', demonstrating for us to see their innate ability.
>
> *Lesley, library visitor*

From the start of the project, the potential to develop creativity with cameras and images became quickly apparent. As educators' confidence grew in their own competencies and because they valued children's own creativity, the children had greater opportunity to take photographs and were found to be motivated by this. Vea Vecchi, atelierista in Reggio Emilia also observes:

> It is truly surprising to see the photographs they take, photographs that let us see their ways of seeing, their totally unanticipated viewpoints, such as the importance they attribute to one colour, filling up an entire photographic image with it ... Ninety per cent of photographs taken by children with digital cameras are details.
>
> *Vecchi 2010, 87*

The legacy of the 'Powerful Images, Powerful Learning' project is far more than just being able to take better photographs. Our ongoing challenge is to make visible what is significant in a child's learning and to offer provocation for future possibilities.

The joy of learning

The significance of Brian's photography project became apparent at the 'Making the Joy of Learning Visible' exhibition held at the MacRobert Arts Centre, Stirling, in November 2010. The exhibition was a celebration of Stirling's ten-year journey into how pedagogical documentation can support young children's learning in the early years. The dynamic action shot selected to publicise the exhibition was chosen for its potential to draw the viewer in, questioning them to consider how and why the image was taken and to challenge perceptions of risk taking. The power of images to create dialogue is what supports the use of the camera as an invaluable tool in documentation.

The context of the image used on the exhibition flyer (see figure on page 74) is summed up in the exhibit title: 'A child's joy as he jumped through the air'. It came about as two educators from Hillview Children and Families' Centre experimented with their new camera and its speed burst function by taking action shots of children jumping outdoors. Two of the educators in particular found working with the children to capture the images was an exciting, joyful experience, where all involved shared in the thrill of discovering something new. Through trying out different settings, and unfamiliar angles, they explored how to create a sense of scale, and where to place things within a frame. Revisiting the images on the computer, and as printed photographs, enabled children to reflect and analyse the differences in their body movements, the shapes they made and their facial

Leap of joy

expressions as they took off, were in mid-air and as they landed. A further significance was the way in which these powerful images stimulated high interest and comment from families; something that one of the educators in particular continues to embrace in his practice:

> The experience provided many meaningful learning opportunities and taught me the value and worth of that one single image that captures the moment a child is totally engaged in learning and discovery.
>
> *Deputy Head, Hillview Children and Families' Centre*

The camera: a vehicle for communication

As the 'Powerful Images, Powerful Learning' project spread out to embrace almost all of Stirling's early years nursery settings, their research work with the digital camera has been disseminated within our wider learning community. One project that holds particular poignancy occurred in Balfron Nursery. The children were invited to become 'eye detectives' and with the aid of magnifiers and cameras to go in search of interesting images in the garden. Three children in particular sustained their interest, and when the photographs were reviewed at the end of the day, the significance of their pictures had a strong impact on their educator. Her insight was based on knowing that all were receiving expressive language support from a Speech and Language Therapist. The focus of the three boys' interest was in taking black and white close ups, suggesting their visual discrimination was enhanced. One of the children, Ethan, made visible his interest in circular objects.

It was as though the camera lens was a 'translator' and could make the three boys' different interests known, without the stress of having to tell others. It was a moment of joy when another of the children, Rory, spoke his first words in nursery: 'It's a spatula', in response to his friends perplexing at the subject of one of his images. For Kate, the educator, the significance of this project came from seeing the boys' anxieties being stripped away as the intimacy of this small group fostered initial interactions and then fluency, as they communicated with others about their work. The Speech and Language Therapist reflected: 'The demands placed upon them to communicate in particular ways can be highly stressful. Holding and being behind the camera had the effect of reducing the pressure on the boys.'

As the project progressed, Ethan's mother observed: 'Such a wonderful insight into how he sees the world. I can now focus with him on details that interest him and talk together. Hearing him chatter with confidence has been rewarding.'

> We see the world as we are, not as it is.
>
> *Goethe*, Faust

This project is a reminder of how we all see and understand the world from different perspectives, and that these can be expressed in many ways. The consideration of images, gestures, and signs in addition to verbal language are some of the many ways children express different viewpoints. Prompting children to think about the validity of all views, tolerance and taking others into consideration, is of equal importance.

During a similar project in Aberfoyle Nursery, in rural Stirlingshire, one of the guiding principles of their encounter with powerful images was to engage with the photography, not just as a means to make learning visible, but as provocation for further discussion and learning, developing in the children the attitudes and skills of debaters. The children are familiar with group discussions reviewing photographs as a way of growing their critical thinking. The richness of learning and the development of thinking and evaluation skills through such opportunities have impacted on the views the children have of their own capacities and competencies, as well as their attitudes to themselves and each other as learners on a shared journey of discovery.

New tools: making learning visible

The power of the video clip

As we continued our exploration of the potential of new technology in supporting children's learning, we made further discoveries. This next section sets out our new understandings of the powerful impact of video clips.

Video clips can be even more powerful than still digital images as they capture the children's excitement and wonder as well as their body actions, gestures and dialogue. Thornton and Brunton (2009, 8) refer to 'Malaguzzi's concept of the hundred languages of expression'; the many ways in which children represent and communicate their interest, thoughts and ideas. In the past, the authors used video cameras to record learning experience onto video tape, but found the amount of material generated was time-consuming to watch and edit. Revisiting particular episodes meant fast forwarding and rewinding back to locate a particular start point of a clip. In recent years, the advent of the pocket camcorder has provided a welcome and much easier to use documentation tool.

Pocket camcorders record and play video clips, and the most convenient have built-in software to edit and organise clips, and a freeze-frame facility to take significant digital images from a video clip. The second major advantage is that they have 'plug and play' technology where an enclosed USB arm connects directly into a USB port so that its own editing software can be installed onto the computer. Pocket camcorders are particularly simple and easy to use with minimal buttons; they are camera sized and can be attached to tripods for safety and more expert videoing.

Since video clips 'listen to' and support children's 'hundred languages', they have great potential to capture aspects of learning that an observer might overlook, such as subtle nuances and expressional behaviours. When replaying video clips it is noticeable how young children appear to focus more on what is happening in the foreground in their discussions. Therefore, getting down to eye level and framing the action is just as important for video as it is with a digital camera.

Slowing down the learning: going deeper

As the pocket camcorder was introduced into settings, many children's interest in new technology saw them keen to try out this new tool for themselves. The simplicity of the camcorder's operation enabled children to use the camera effectively and, with the aid of the tripod, safely. Some of the children's first video clips in Stirling recorded small groups of children retelling well known stories such as 'Handa's Surprise', 'Goldilocks' and the 'Billy Goats Gruff'. Often multiple re-runs of the same story allowed children to practice taking turns in being the narrator, puppeteer and camera crew. Forman (1999) refers to the potential of the video camera as a 'memory machine' since 'instant video replaying' gives an accurate account of a particular activity, allowing groups of children to critically reflect upon and assess their own, and others' filming techniques. The benefits of the plug and play technology enabled instant transfer onto the laptop or Smart Board, where children could see and evaluate even the smallest details, often leading to suggestions about how to improve their filming technique. What is impressive is the ease with which groups of children have been able to edit and sequence short clips and then drag them into a movie. Each movie demonstrated how the puppeteers collaborated as they retold stories, weaving together the actions of the characters, dialogue and body language, which in another media would have been lost.

Children and adults as researchers

Working across a number of settings, the nursery teacher (pedagogista) in Stirling is able to engage in, encourage and support small-scale action research into the potential of newer technologies and their effectiveness in promoting children's learning. In this example, the pocket camcorder supported adult and children's co-construction of meaning as they engaged in a series of rocket trials to answer the children's own question: 'How do rockets fly?'

At Cornton Nursery, a Space Learning Group had formed after a number of children had expressed interest in planets and rockets. The educators respectively engaged in this action research project in which the more experienced of them worked collaboratively with the other to take forward thinking and practice so that, in future, she could lead a similar project alongside another educator. Both educators approached this project with no preconceived plan about the direction in which it ought to go. Instead, they initiated a culture of 'listening and responding' amongst the educator and children, where opportunities were created to share ideas and thinking. Although there are many excellent information books and Internet sites to research knowledge about space, the educators believed that merely transferring facts to the children would not automatically lead to conceptual understanding. Underpinning their belief was their appreciation of John Dewey's theories that 'children learn by doing' and that 'experimentation and independent thinking should be fostered' (quoted in Pound 2005, 21). They recognised that one of their roles within the learning group would be as researchers, seeking out possible experiments that would enable children to be active in their own learning journey of discovery.

'How do rockets fly?' became the provocation for the Learning Group. Together, the children and adults researched possible experiments using the Internet. With the adults acting in a collaborative role to distil what might be possible. The group decided to try out an experiment in which Alka Seltzer mixed with water served as rocket fuel. By adjusting the proportions of water and Alka Seltzer one rocket finally took off and reached five metres high within two to three seconds. The flight happened so quickly that the slow shutter speed of the digital camera missed the event entirely, and the pocket camcorder recorded just a few seconds of rocket flight. The children's delight at how the rocket had flown upwards was evident. Understandably, their initial comments were concerned with how fast and how far the successful rocket travelled rather than with their bigger question of how rockets fly into space. The educators were astonished that the two second clip contained enough frames to show the top of the lid being blown off the tube, followed by a stream of fizz as the rocket took off. Cropping the image brought the framed action to the forefront and put the child at the centre of the experience again. The children's dialogue seems to have been enriched by being able to pause the video at significant points and to see the experiments in slow motion, several times over.

When the space group first formed, children found it hard to focus on another child's interest, drawing, question or idea. By bouncing their thoughts off each other, they generated new theories. The technology provided by the pocket camcorder enabled children to 'see again', to reflect and to suggest how and why some rockets flew and others did not. The powerful images taken from the video provoked further dialogue, with both children and families, about what had happened and why.

Another practical aspect of the pocket camcorder is that, in the playroom, it is a multi-purpose tool. In addition to 'seeing' the action, narratives and questioning are all recorded with the facility to extract digital stills of significant moments. This highlights the pocket camcorder's potential as a worthwhile documentation tool, particularly when an educator is working alone with a group of children and has to make a choice about the best tool to choose.

New technologies in the daily life of a setting

Small digital cameras and pocket camcorders are unobtrusive and as such provide a good way for educators to observe children in their play without halting the flow of their different interactions. Many nurseries make use of short video clips to support the daily life of the setting. Digital cameras record good video footage that can be transferred via memory card to the laptop instantly. There are a number of possibilities.

Video clips facilitate professional dialogue exploring the effectiveness of play opportunities and resourcing. In this way the educator's reflections are less subjective and fewer assumptions are made about how the learning environment is being used. This approach supports change when needed and improved practice across the team and individually. An educator from Aberfoyle Nursery made an additional observation about how the pocket camcorder can be used to boost professional development.

> Another good use [of the pocket camcorder] is when we get other professionals in, because you don't always remember what they do. We filmed John from Active Stirling and he's brilliant with the children. Having the video meant we could look at it with the children and they would see themselves and remember. It would also remind us what he did so we could take it forward and practice between sessions.
>
> *Elaine, Aberfoyle Nursery*

Video clips demonstrate how individual children respond to different experiences in the nursery, and can be especially valuable in providing feedback to educators, parents or visiting professionals about how a child is settling into a setting. They have the capacity to reassure, as they make visible social interactions that give an indication of a child's wellbeing, their involvement in what the setting has to offer and the beginnings of forming friendships. An educator from Raploch Nursery, used short video clips very effectively to document the progress of a child who arrived at nursery with no spoken English. The educator puzzled over how to build a learning journal that would be meaningful to Alperen and his family, none of whom were able to read or speak any significant English. The educator decided to use her creative abilities with Windows Movie Maker to record short, daily

Blast off

video clips to reassure his family that he was happy, taking part in a range of activities, and beginning to interact with children and adults. The educator's key group became her aides, with the children often alerting her to some significant learning of Alperen's that they thought she should capture. The most significant clips were compiled onto a DVD and given to Alperen when he moved away from Raploch. This has positively influenced the practice of other educators and teachers of English as an Additional Language.

New technologies: a new confidence

Children are becoming increasingly familiar with and adept at using a variety of technology at an early age. Lewis, at three years old, has met and enthusiastically overcome the challenges of working with three generations of computer technology. He confidently works between them, and on occasions, even combines them. When Lewis started to use the Windows programme on the laptop at Crianlarich Nursery, he tried to operate the functions by touching the screen. He was used to working with a touchscreen as at home and was a competent, confident user of his parents' iPad. Lewis mastered using the touch pad to move the cursor and educators queried whether or not to introduce him to a mouse, now 'old hat' in technology terms. This they did as he might need to use one when he moved to school. The educators need not have worried; Lewis now chooses to attach a mouse to a laptop and can be seen at times with one hand on the touch pad and the mouse in the other moving between them with deftness and skill. Although to adults the rapidly changing technology can be a hurdle, it is less so to children who embrace challenges as they meet them.

As the performance of tablets has risen, and the price has become more affordable, their potential as a documentation and research tool has been realised by a number of nursery settings. Although their size makes them more intrusive and unwieldy than a pocket camcorder or video camera, tablets are becoming more popular as they have other benefits. Tablets provide instant playback of stills and videos on a screen that is large enough for a small group to gather around for a discussion. In the figure opposite, Lewis and Alfie scroll through digital images of a squirrel raiding the nut feeders at Crianlarich Nursery. Being more portable than a laptop tablets can facilitate instant group learning indoors and out. The intimacy of gathering around the screen encourages investigation in a relaxed and natural way, inviting children to hypothesize, question and reflect on their learning together. Additionally, they can be connected to other devices for larger audiences.

Further advantages of tablets are that digital images and videos can be stored, edited and shared using the same device, without having to plug them into a computer. The files can also be emailed or shared via Bluetooth to a compatible destination for storing or printing. This does depend on the availability of a WiFi connection, which is usually not a problem in urban areas but is more challenging in rural settings such as Crianlarich where the signal strength is more intermittent. When WiFi is not available, tablets can be plugged into a computer and the images downloaded in a similar way as for a digital camera.

The responsiveness of tablets, with their various applications, offers children a visual and tactile experience as they use the tool to interact and represent the world around them. Art applications facilitate free movement with fingers, which provide both a co-ordination and sensory experience. Through these art programs, children can incorporate an array of virtual colour and textural media such as oil paint and pastel, which might not ordinarily be physically available, on a variety of backgrounds including photographs. A stylus allows even

Alfie and Lewis with the iPad

greater finesse and feels like a pen or pencil as children practice mark making, drawing and writing.

The touchscreen technology allows children to get the feel for shapes and objects by allowing them to trace around shapes before attempting to draw freehand on paper. This encourages children to experiment and 'have a go', but for some young artists it allows them to 'undo' a stroke or line, giving them another chance to coordinate what they are creating with what is in their head. This can boost confidence and give individual children the freedom to experiment without the fear of failure. This is very important for some children who according to Dweck (2012) 'may have a perfectionist streak or "closed mindset", which restricts their willingness to be innovative'.

Concluding thoughts

Working across a number of settings, the nursery teacher (pedagogista) in Stirling is able to engage in, encourage and support small-scale action research into the potential of newer technologies and their effectiveness in promoting children's learning. The use of these new technologies provides additional, improved and sometimes faster ways of sharing or provoking learning. Carr and Lee (2012, 118) comment on the work of Kress, who considers that these new technologies add to the more traditional, written text that 'tell the world', extending the boundaries to 'depicted and displayed' texts that 'show the world'.

Children are motivated by different technologies, and as they are gaining in confidence in using them, they are increasingly taking ownership of their learning and how they go about making their learning visible. We as teachers and educators in the early years must keep doors open by embracing these technologies in order to support children in a technological future that we cannot yet envisage. We must not be fearful of what might come or go; children adapt and combine different technologies according to their needs and curiosities. Our role is to provide opportunities to experience and to make visible children's many languages.

In only fifteen years, the authors have recorded the children's learning using a progression of different technologies from Polaroid and film, floppy discs and magnetic tape, memory cards and USB pens, to portable hard drives and cloud storage. Our successes and failures in archiving significant learning encounters have led us to give careful consideration to how we are saving digital materials for archiving. By keeping the original text, image or clip in their purest format we believe there is more chance of reproducing them with quality, using any technology the future presents us with.

Chapter 7

Taking documentation into primary school

Tanya Starkey

Callander Primary School, with a school roll of 220, sits within the rural town of Callander, which serves as the eastern gateway to the Loch Lomond and the Trossachs National Park and is a popular tourist stop to and from the Highlands of Scotland. The school includes a nursery class offering morning and afternoon places, a mainstream school covering stages Primary 1 to Primary 7 and an Autistic Spectrum Disorder Provision.[1] The majority of our nursery children enrol into Primary 1 at our school and the school is owned and maintained by Stirling Council. The school and nursery are the only educational settings within the town and therefore play an important role within the community.

At Callander Primary School we have a passion for developing enthusiastic life-long learners who set high expectations for themselves and others. Within our setting our nursery team members have embraced the principles of the Reggio Emilio approach to learning, which are deeply embedded into all aspects of nursery life. As educators working within the Early level of Curriculum for Excellence (Scottish National Curriculum Approach) whose principles are an expression of pedagogical documentation we were keen to develop this approach as the children moved in to the primary school. This sets the background to our involvement in a project that promoted the importance of smooth, effective transitions from nursery into Primary 1.

Previous to our involvement in the 'Making Learning Visible in Primary 1' project we had a well-established transition programme in place for nursery to Primary 1. This programme included opportunities for the nursery children to regularly access the classrooms and other key areas of the main school building. There were also opportunities for the children to meet their Primary 1 teachers and visit the classrooms and have lunch within the school dining hall. All nursery children were assigned a Primary 7 buddy who had received training from the Learning Support teacher within the school. There had been some transition project work undertaken in the form of a summer holiday booklet to be completed by the children in the holiday preceding the first term of Primary 1. Other transition activities included filling a treasure box with holiday memories to be made into posters in the first few days of Primary 1. The emphasis of these transition opportunities was always placed on the children's emotional, mental and physical well-being and although we received very positive feedback from the parents of the nursery children with regard to their child's move to Primary 1 we felt that there was a need to establish a new layer to the transition process that focused not just on the physical move to school but also on the progression of the children's learning.

It was essential, through discussion with the nursery team, for the Primary 1 teachers to understand and be aware that each nursery child was coming to school with their own individual skills, areas of knowledge and stages of development and that each child should be given opportunities to develop their learning at their own pace. If we were going to build on the Reggio approach, so firmly established within our nursery setting, we needed the Primary 1 team to understand that children are capable of constructing their own learning and that they can develop an understanding of themselves and their place in the world through their interactions with others.

> Children are naturally curious and eager to find out about the world around them. We must build on their curiosity and enthusiasm to learn when we develop their learning environments, working outwards from their individual interests and needs.
>
> *HMIE Scotland 2007, 4*

As a result of this shared understanding between the nursery and Primary 1 team it was agreed that in the last term before summer the nursery team would identify the children's key learning interests that had naturally evolved within the nursery setting and would share these interests with the Primary 1 teachers. At this point the whole early level team (nursery and Primary 1) would decide which of these themes of enquiry and interests could be developed into a transition project beginning in nursery and continuing into the first term of Primary 1.

It was with some trepidation that we embarked on this new way of learning. A number of challenges were ahead of us, such as organising times for whole team planning, ensuring ways of incorporating the children's learning interests and looking at how this new way of planning may have an impact on whole school planning. However, with all this in mind we commenced discussions and planning.

The first year of trialling this new approach began by developing the children's interest in animals and the enjoyment of the story of *The Gruffalo*. The story was introduced within the nursery setting with some work on the characters through writing and expressive arts, which was further developed in Primary 1 with a focus on the forest, forest animals and the seasons. This was a successful first step with the children sharing their ideas and pieces of work with the nursery team once they had moved into the primary setting. This was a good start to a new way of effective, continuous learning for the children.

The most recent transition project was agreed within the early level team as having a focus on castles as this was an area of interest to a large group of nursery children within the last term. The nursery team focused on building castles using junk materials and castle life using various images of real and imaginary castles. It was decided that this project could be further developed within Primary 1 by moving the children's learning towards fairy castles with a focus on fairy stories.

At this point it was discussed that not all nursery children had shown an interest in castles and had therefore not developed their understanding of castles or had not undertaken focused junk modelling activities whilst at nursery. We also had children coming to join us in Primary 1 who had attended other nurseries and had therefore not had the same opportunities perhaps as other children to research castles. It was agreed then that within Primary

1, as well as the fairy castles and stories activities, all children would be given opportunities to develop an interest in castles and a focus would also be placed on the skills incorporated into effective discussion, observational drawing and modelling.

Once the children had started Primary 1 the castle project began to take shape and evolve. Although the original theme for the learning context had been identified by the early level team we felt it was important as the mentors and guides for the children to engage all children in all stages of planning. We were keen to provide stimulating, interesting activities that were not only planned by the children but also then engaged them in such a way that they would want to explore and investigate independently. We were beginning to incorporate an understanding of the 100 languages of children as implicit in the Reggio approach to children's learning.

We therefore planned the fairy castle project with the children. They could tell us which story characters they thought could live in Fairyland and it was from these early discussions with the children that specific fairy story characters and stories were further developed within the class. With the knowledge shared between the nursery team and Primary 1 teachers of the children's understanding and skills developed within nursery along with the evaluations of the children's discussions we were able to establish and identify several strands of learning to be taken forward.

The skills and knowledge identified in nursery were further developed through the children participating in tasks using junk modelling, for example, making a picnic basket for Red Riding Hood and using junk materials and commercially produced technology kits to build imaginary castles.

We also provided opportunities for the children to develop their literacy skills through listening to, recalling, retelling and sequencing their favourite fairy stories. Early writing was encouraged by giving the children opportunities to label and describe characters from the stories. Problem-solving challenges were set such as sorting and organising furniture for the Three Bears' cottage and creating an imaginary fairy tale castle using two-dimensional shapes.

Once the learning context had been established and planned for, we then focused on strategies to develop a way of making the children's learning visible following on from the documentation approach embedded into nursery practice. Due to the fact that within our Primary 1 the ratio of children to adults this session is 17:1 (last session it was 25:1), it was challenging to find ways in which we could document the children's learning in the same format and quantity as our nursery. We trialled a variety of strategies including photography, video, observation, scribing and discussion as ways to assess, evaluate and record the children's learning and experiences. The most powerful of these strategies, we have found, is discussion with the children. As we engage in dialogue with the children we are made aware not just of their learning but also their understanding of their learning. The children are able to state what their achievements are and, crucially, discuss with us where they think their learning journey should take them next. Significant examples of work and a record of the discussion are placed into the children's profiles. These are shared with parents regularly and parents are encouraged to contribute their thoughts to the profiles also. The class teachers would also use this evidence and information to assess the children's learning in order to inform future planning and further develop learning across the curriculum.

One member of the Primary 1 team has identified how her practice has evolved and adapted since working so closely with the nursery team. She adds that over the last few years of working this way the learning taking place in the class has been shaped in many ways by the children's interests and current understanding, which ultimately has made for a range of different experiences for each group of children.

In order to make the classroom environment an effective space for learning we did not want to impose seating restrictions upon the children, therefore the children do not have fixed seats or places to work in the classroom. They are free to work where and with whom they wish, which allows significant opportunities for co-operative and collaborative working with each other. However, at times, from an educator's perspective, it can be challenging to manage the activities and tasks as well as find quality time to spend with each child to record their ideas, thoughts and learning. It was decided that the most appropriate and effective use of time would be to have focus groups of children within each task where the rest of the class would be given small tasks to complete independently. This allowed greater time for the teacher to focus on individual learners. By having these small focus groups the class teachers were able to use all of the above strategies to record significant learning and ideas.

> Learners who are helped to engage positively in conversations about:
> how they are doing;
> where they want to go; and
> what they need to get there
> have an increased chance of continuing to learn and strengthening their own leadership for learning.
>
> *Education Scotland 2009, 52*

Throughout the first term in Primary 1 the class teachers continually evaluated the strategies used to document the learning along with the effectiveness of the transition project. Although the documentation may look and feel slightly different in Primary 1, all teachers involved felt that the time spent with the children during these focused learning times was invaluable. Formative assessment information gathered at these times continually fed into termly, weekly and daily planning in order to provide the children with suitable support or challenge. This led to the children accessing resources and progressing in their learning at a pace appropriate to them.

At school and authority level we believe that transition to school is a major event in the lives of young children which needs to be carefully planned for and supported. As one parent commented on our transition work:

> The transition programme was a huge benefit to my son. In particular the visits during the school year meant that he was very confident about starting school as there were far less unknown elements and the project was a good way of allowing my son to share his interests with the Primary 1 staff.

By ensuring the child is at the centre of planning for a transition project, along with a variety of other planned events and encounters, we feel the children are able to make a smooth transition from nursery to school. As a team we recognise that the visibility of the children's learning is different to that of the nursery but what we have understood is that this is appropriate since it recognises and accepts the difference between a nursery setting and a school environment. The most important elements are the same; the principles of the Reggio approach to learning have been embraced and implemented, which is the most important aspect of this way of working and although the visibility may be different we have adapted and developed ways of learning and teaching that build upon the sound foundations the learners experience in nursery. We have not found it an easy journey and we certainly do not have all of the answers but we feel we have given the children a sense of belonging, purpose and an environment where all ideas and thoughts are listened to. We have worked hard to find ways of representing the learning that is manageable and sustainable and our reservations and those of others that working with this approach could mean that children would not be at the level required for the next stage in the primary school have been unfounded. We celebrate this and look forward to continuing and building upon our work in the future with our whole early years team working in collaboration with each other.

Note

1   Primary 1 in Scotland is the first class in primary school, following immediately on from nursery setting.

Chapter 8

Making learning visible

Pedagogical documentation: sustaining this approach

Linda Kinney

Reflections

In our previous book, *An Encounter with Reggio Emilia*, we reflected in our final chapter on the issues that faced us at that point on our journey. We set out what we believed were our next steps in the development of a whole authority model of pedagogical documentation. In this final chapter, we thought it would be a good opportunity to reflect and to consider 'what happens next' as a result of what we know now, and how best can we sustain this model in the future?

In writing, editing and collaborating on this book, one powerful resonance is the unique quality of the 'voices' in each of the chapters. The authors reflecting on their individual journeys, sharing their stories, capturing their understandings and thinking, provides us with compelling insights into their individual learning and importantly, together, provides us with a collective understanding and knowledge of the development of pedagogical documentation across the Stirling Council area.

It is this collective understanding that offers a frame of work to help us to think more deeply about what we have learned about pedagogical documentation.

What are these key collective understandings?

In the introduction, Pat set out what we have understood about the practice of pedagogical documentation. In this final chapter, I am setting out our key strategic understandings, in order to help us to consider what we need to do next.

Although these key understandings are not necessarily new, they are an indication of our current thinking and priorities at this stage including what we have learned about ourselves.

• We have continued to learn that at its heart, documentation is about 'knowing the person', the starting point is who we are as human beings, who we are as people, our differences as well as our similarities. This means that we need to know the child as a person in the context of their home and family and not only as a learner in an early years setting.

- The immense capability of children continues to inspire us, and more visible now is the immense capability of adults in their collaborations with children. Pedagogical documentation has made adult learning and its potential more visible.
- The central importance of home and family in making early learning visible to a wider community and audience. Although we have always understood the importance of home and family in supporting children's learning, the impact and potential of the family to be a 'tipping point' for a wider community that understands the capabilities of young children has become more evident.
- The critical importance of leadership, particularly in sustaining this way of thinking and working.

What does this mean for what happens next?

Our starting point is to ask some *key questions*:

- If knowing who we are as people is critical to helping us to know others, including children, then *how best do we support and encourage adults to understand and learn more about themselves?* How best do we help adults to know their possibilities, their impact on others?
- How best can we connect to and harness the energy, talents and experience of our local communities in progressing the pedagogical documentation approach?
- In a context that is constantly changing, what kind of leadership and leaders do we need to sustain this approach? What are the knowledge and skills required in progressing and sustaining the pedagogical documentation approach?

The new understandings that we now have continue to show us the powerful impact not only on children, but also on adults and communities in making early learning visible and working with a model of pedagogical documentation. In changing times, how best we can sustain this model in the future?

Considerations

It is well documented (Grint and Brooks 2010, and in other publications) that we are facing a time of unprecedented change in society, e.g. complex social problems around the education, care and well-being of children, the global financial crisis and in particular its impact on public services, including early years provision.

Stirling Council, as with all other local councils in Scotland, is facing major reductions in funding available for local services. Difficult decisions are being taken locally by politicians in consultation with communities to identify spending priorities. The outcome is that some service areas will continue to be supported and funded, whilst other service areas will be reduced and possibly removed. The decisions made by our politicians are critical to the continued development of early years provision.

In Stirling, all political parties have stated their commitment to early years provision and have announced their decision (in February 2014) to continue to fund early years at existing levels and in some areas to enhance opportunities for developing provision.

Nationally, the Scottish Government has pledged to 'improve the lives of young children in Scotland'. It aims to achieve this by introducing new legislation that creates an obligation on future governments (in Scotland), on local councils and health services to deliver early years services and to view such services as an essential part of a child/young person's 'learning journey'.

> What happens to children in their earliest years says much about our society and is key to outcomes in adult life'
>
> *Scottish Government 2008, 8*

The Scottish Government's Early Years Framework 2008 provides the basis for a new vision for early years in Scotland. It has at its core a recognition of the importance of providing the best possible opportunities for our youngest children. It believes the best way to achieve this is to work in partnership across agencies and communities to ensure that children are valued and provided for within communities. The Scottish Government has also established the Early Years Collaborative (2013). The objective of the collaborative is to transform the principles set out in the Early Years Framework into actions.

The stated ambitions and commitments set out in the Early Years Framework and the Collaborative provide solid foundations to ensure that the early years remain a priority in Scotland and in Stirling. This is significant in terms of sustaining the documentation approach as it gives out a strong message about the importance of young children in our society and ensuring that we make available the best possible provisions.

Sustaining pedagogical documentation: some ingredients

Our experience in Stirling has shown us that developing and sustaining pedagogical documentation requires people who are committed to and understand the importance of early learning. The success in Stirling of developing a whole authority approach owes a great deal to the courage and leadership of the early years team at the centre of the organisation, who worked in a developmental and transformational way with the early years settings. The political and strategic leadership at the highest level of the organisation was also a key factor in our success.

In developing and sustaining the documentation approach in Stirling we have understood that the following key ingredients have been significant.

1   Leadership: political, strategic, local
2   Knowledge and understanding
3   Children first

Leadership

> It is what the vision does, rather than what it says. It is what we do, not only what we say that will make the real difference.
>
> *Stirling Council's 'Framework for Leadership'*

Political leadership

From the outset, the strong political lead and belief in early years has ensured that each political party and the leader of the council was active in promoting, developing and supporting a model of early years provision based on pedagogical documentation. Stirling Council received national recognition for the outstanding performance of the early years settings in the national Education Inspections (HMIE) of early learning and for the way in which early years was being developed. This level of recognition provided an opportunity for political as well as strategic leaders in Stirling to contribute to and influence thinking and policy development in early years provision in Scottish Government.

Strategic leadership

We believe that Stirling benefited from having at the highest level of the organisation, within Education (the Head of Education) and then at a corporate organisational level (Assistant Chief Executive) an individual with an understanding of and commitment to developing a model of early years provision and practice based on pedagogical documentation. This was significant in providing strategic leadership throughout the organisation, in sharing knowledge and experience, being able to share the histories of the provision and to influence politicians, locally and nationally of the importance of early learning.

Local leadership

The development of integrated nurseries, such as Park Drive, Croftamie and Raploch as outlined in the previous chapters, provided a critical source of local leadership. Heads of nurseries, knowledgeable about early learning, were able to provide leadership and management at a local community level. Some head teachers in schools with nursery classes attached, who became knowledgeable about early learning and pedagogical documentation, were also an important source of leadership. When this local leadership of early years provision combined with the early years development and management team at the centre of the organisation it was a powerful and influential group in ensuring our theoretic understandings could happen in practice. It was in these settings, where a critical mass of early learning practice developed, that we came to the position where the practice and theory merged.

Knowledge and understanding

> A people without the knowledge of their past history, origin and culture is like a tree without root.
>
> *Marcus Garvey*

Understanding our past thinking and practice in relation to children and early learning is crucial in understanding our present thinking and practice. Understanding why the documentation approach is not only a pedagogical model, but is an approach that is life-affirming and in its creation an 'act of love', requires people who have, and/or are willing to develop and grow, their current knowledge and understanding about early learning and about themselves.

Bibliography

Berger, J. (1972) *Ways of Seeing*, Penguin.

Boyd Cadwell, L. (2003) *Bringing Learning to Life: The Reggio Approach in Early Childhood Education*, Teachers College Press.

Bridges, W. (2011) *Managing Transitions*, Nicholas Brearly Publishing.

Bruner, J. (2011) *Wonder of Learning, Hundred Languages of Children*, Reggio Children.

Cahn, E. (2004) *No More Throw-Away People: The Co-Production Imperative*, 2nd Edition, Essential Books.

Carr, M. (2001) *Assessment in Early Childhood Settings: Learning Stories*, Paul Chapman.

Carr, M. and Lee, W. (2012) *Learning Stories: Constructing Learner Identities in Early Education*. Sage.

Ceppi, G. and Zini, M. (1998) *Children, Spaces, Relations: Metaproject for an Environment for Young Children*, Reggio Children.

Clark, A., Kjorhold A.T. and Moss, P. (eds) (2005) *Beyond Listening*, Policy Press.

Clark, A. and Moss, P. (2001) *Listening to Young Children. The Mosaic Approach*, National Children's Bureau.

Curtis, S.J. and Boultwood, M.E.A. (1963) *A Short History of Educational Ideas*, Cambridge University Press. Dahlberg, G. (1999) 'Reflections on the Reggio Emilia experience', in H. Penn (ed.) *Early Childhood Services*, Chapter 11, Open University Press.

Dahlberg, G and Moss, P. (2005) *Ethics and Politics in Early Childhood Education*, Routledge Falmer.

Dahlberg, G., Moss, P. and Pence, A. (1999) *Beyond Quality in Early Childhood Education and Care: Post Modern Perspectives*, Falmer Press.

Dahlberg. G, Moss P. and Pence A., (2007) *Beyond Quality in Early Childhood Education and Care Languages of Evaluation*, 2nd edn, Routledge.

Donaldson, M. (1987) *Children's Minds*, Fontana Press.

Donaldson, M., Grieve, R. and Pratt, C. (eds) (1983) *Early Childhood Development and Education*, Blackwell.

Dunn, R. (1998) *Anne Bruetsch's Multiple Intelligences Lesson Plan Book*, Zephyr Press.

Dweck, C. S. (2012*) Mindset: How You Can Fulfil Your Potential*, Robinson.

Education Scotland (2009) *Early Years Leadership for Learning*, Education Scotland.

Ewing, R. (2010) *The Arts and Australian Education: Realising Potential*, Australian Council for Education Research.

Fletcher-Watson, B. (2013) 'Child's play: A postdramatic theatre of *Paidia* for the very young', *Platform*, 'Staging Play, Playing Stages', 7(2).

Friere, P. (1972) *Pedagogy of the Oppressed*, Penguin.

Forman, G. (1999) 'Instant video: Revisiting the video camera as "A tool of the mind" for young children', *Early Childhood Research Practice*, 1(2).

Fortunati, A. (2006) *The Education of Young Children as a Community Project*, Edizione Junior.

Gandini, L. and Pope Edwards, C. (eds) (2001) *Bambini: The Italian Approach to Infant/ Toddler Care*, Teachers College Press.

Giudici, C., Krechevsky, M. and Rinaldi, C. (2001) *Making Children's Early Learning Visible: Children as Individual and Group Learners*, Project Zero and Reggio Children.

Giudici, C. and Vecchi, V. (2004) *Children, Art, Artists: The Expressive Languages of Children, The Artistic Language of Alberto Burri*, Reggio Children.

Greig, E. (2002) 'A documentation approach to early learning', Action Research Paper, Dundee University.

Greig, E. (2003) 'Impact of dissemination programme within Stirling Council Early Childhood Services', Action Research Paper, Dundee University.

Grint, K. (2007) 'The arts of leadership', Cranfield University, School of Management: Knowledge Interchange Podcast. Available online at: www.som.cranfield.ac.uk/som/ dinamic-content/media/knowledgeinterchange/booksummaries/Arts%20of%20 Leadership%20-%20Part%201/Transcript.pdf (last accessed 20 November, 2014).

Grint, K. and Brooks, S. (2010) *The New Public Leadership Challenge*, Palgrave MacMillan.

Hallett, C. and Prout, A. (2003) *Hearing the Voices of Children: Social Policy for a New Century*, Routledge Falmer.

HMIE Scotland (2007) *Child at the Centre: Self-Evaluation in the Early Years*, HM Inspectorate of Education.

HMIE (2010) 'A Report by HM Inspectorate of Education and the Care Commission: Doune Nursery', HM Inspectorate of Education.

Hull, K., Goldhaber, J. and Capone, A. (2001) *Opening Doors*, Houghton Mifflin.

Kinney, L. and Wharton, P. (2008) *An Encounter with Reggio Emilia: Children's Early Learning Made Visible*, Routledge.

Krechevsky, M. (2001) 'Form, function, and understanding in learning groups: propositions from the reggio classrooms', in C. Giudici, C. Rinaldi and M. Krechevsky (eds), *Making Learning Visibile: Children as Individual and Group Learners* (pp. 246–69), Project Zero and Reggio Children.

Krechevsky, A., Mardell, B., Melissa, R. and Wilson, D. (2013) *Visible Learners: Promoting Reggio Inspired Approaches in All Schools*, Jossey-Bass.

Lancaster, Y. P. (2003) *Listening to Young Children*, Open University Press.

Lansdown, G. (2005) *Can you Hear Me? The Right of Young Children to Participate in Decisions Affecting Them*, Bernard Van Leer Foundation.

Learning, Teaching Scotland (2005) *Let's Talk about Pedagogy*, Learning, Teaching Scotland.

Malaguzzi, L. *et al.* (1987) *The Hundred Languages of Children: Narrative of the Possible*. Reggio Emilia: Department of Education.

Creating a new dynamic: a new collaborative

The model of developing and supporting pedagogical documentation that we described earlier, particularly around the leadership elements, could be described as a fairly traditional hierarchical approach. The change to this model leaves an opportunity. It offers room or space for another model of leadership or elements of the existing leadership model to emerge.

> Leadership is not like following a cooking recipe, because the ingredients that leaders use are not dead, but live, not compliant, but resistant. There are no seven ways to guaranteed success because there are not guarantees.
>
> *Grint 2007*

One of the key insights that we have gleaned as part of writing and collaborating on this book is the tremendous capability of the adults based in the early years settings who are in collaboration with children and families, and increasingly with communities.

We will continue to have local leaders and heads of nurseries with the knowledge and experience of pedagogical documentation. Working together, these leaders can themselves become a collaborative. Collaborative leadership means working together in a way that recognises and understands the differences as well as similarities of each leader. It requires leaders to understand one another and to understand what is important individually as well as collectively. Working collaboratively and agreeing what is possible to 'create together' has the potential to increase significantly the capacity and ability of this 'team of leaders'.

This new collaborative leadership has the potential to respond to the key questions set out earlier in the chapter. By coming together in a leadership collaborative they can organise their provisions to make space available for personal and professional development, they can use their influence with key people in key positions in the organisation to gain the space and times and if necessary the resources to achieve this. They are also in a key position along with their own professional teams, to harness the potential of family and community, extending their collaborations to include family and community in a way that helps them to understand and support pedagogical documentation, as an effective way to extend our knowledge and understanding of this way of thinking and working with children. Importantly, it takes this understanding beyond the boundaries of the institution of the early years setting and into the wider community. By working together to find the best way of doing this and by sharing their own successes with each other, this would provide a good starting point.

In this new dynamic, there is an opportunity for a new group to emerge that could be central in leading and supporting the progression of the knowledge, skills and research opportunities around pedagogical documentation. Our vision to transform the role of the nursery teacher, more towards the role of pedagogista, has been set in motion. Changes to the organisation and focus for nursery teachers has been established, moving from a role based on managerial responsibilities towards an approach that is about 'leading learning'. There is an opportunity for this group of nursery teachers to continue to develop and transform their role further, to become the new pedagogistas, and to work as a collaborative. Their current roles and responsibilities put them in a central position in leading learning alongside the nursery heads. Helping to create opportunities for dialogue, debate for action research and sharing this across the early years settings and the wider education service would contribute to the creation of the space and place for professionals to extend their knowledge and practice. Working together to find a collective voice, becoming a collective 'expert', contributing to the wider education debates, dialogue and policy developments, would ensure that the knowledge and experience in early years was being heard and felt beyond the early years settings. Taking a lead role in reading and researching, including national and international developments, would ensure the 'expert' scaffolding of learning continues. This collaborative could assist in ensuring that a supported framework for professional development of all early years professionals continued.

One of the key features of progressing the pedagogical documentation approach in Stirling, at almost every stage, has been the courage, conviction and ability of key people to push beyond existing boundaries. This approach will continue to be sustained and to grow if we continue to have the courage and conviction.

When this courage and conviction of the people who are currently working with pedagogical documentation is combined with the clear political support for early years in Stirling and Scotland, we can, we think, be optimistic about the future.

If we have no money, all we have is each other, now that's true abundance!

Dr Edgar Cahn (masterclass, Stirling Council 2011)

Having high aspirations and expectations of our early years professionals were strong values in Stirling. Alongside these values, we believed, was a responsibility on us to support, encourage and, where appropriate, to nurture our early years professionals to achieve their potential.

Encouraging early years professionals to gain additional qualifications, to attend ongoing professional development, to be part of professional dialogue networks and to take time and make space to reflect on our understandings, were core to the way in which we developed our thinking and learning. We actively sought out opportunities for early years professionals to share practice and to talk to other professionals in other local authorities in Scotland and internationally. We created opportunities for professionals to engage in action research and also to be part of an international research network as we believe the skills and practice associated with taking part in action research is beneficial for personal and professional learning.

The involvement of a local consultant and expert with knowledge and experience of pedagogical documentation, along with Carlina Rinaldi, provided a focus and inspiration for our professional learning and development. The local development of a pedagogical documentation modular training programme that supports early educators and others in their continuous professional development, has been critical to expanding and developing our knowledge and understanding of this way of thinking and working

Writing down, recording our understandings either as part of our policy guidance, or as projects to share, has ensured that we are able to trace our histories, our journey and our thinking. This has been an important element of building our knowledge and understandings to share with each other and with others beyond Stirling. Our documentation has supported us in our reflections and has enabled us to build on previous understandings or indeed develop 'new branches' as we continue to grow our pedagogical documentation approach. These documents, including this book, also help to spread our knowledge and understanding of the amazing capabilities of children and, more obvious now, the professional adults collaborating with children.

Putting children first

This may sound clichéd today, but in 1996 our first early childhood policy report entitled 'Children First', heralded at that time a new way of talking and thinking about children in Stirling. It was a controversial title even then, partly because there was concern from some people that it would be tokenistic. Social services colleagues were concerned that it missed out 'families' and for some it seemed trite. Many conversations and debates have taken place throughout the years and the act of having these conversations was part of the change in thinking. The conversations allowed people to talk to each other, and in the talking we could begin to explore our values base, how we understood children in the context of society, the family and in our professional role. This enabled us to be able to construct some core values and principles that we could agree on, or sign up to in our thinking and work with children and families. These became the starting point of all policy and guidance documents developed around our early years practice and have provided a reference point for early years professionals and others.

Putting children first also meant that we needed to 'give voice' to children, to hear children's voices and to have children's voices heard alongside adult voices. This also was a controversial stage in developing our pedagogical documentation approach and became a highly political issue. Some adults were concerned that their voice would be diminished. Some adults were so concerned that their power base would be reduced that they engaged in behaviours designed to undermine children's voices and decisions based on children's understandings. Some adults revered children's voices and held these voices as the most precious voice beyond all other voices. We think that these were necessary stages for people to pass through in coming to an understanding about the power struggle in our relationship with children, and to be able to move towards an understanding of what it means, what it looks like and feels like for adults and children to be in collaboration.

Consulting with and collaborating with children, although embedded in early years settings, remains controversial beyond early years setting.

What does this tell us for what we need to do next?

> Change can become the medium of exchange, if we change the characteristics we change the dynamic.
>
> *Cahn 2004*

We have established that the commitment to early years provisions politically is in place but that challenges will remain as changes take place around these provisions. We also know that challenges can be opportunities, and that our fear of change can sometimes prevent us from seeing the new dynamic.

Some changing characteristics

Currently in Stirling, in line with most other local authorities in Scotland, early years provision sits within the Education Service. The leadership development and quality of the early years service is therefore led by the education management team.

Changes in the overall organisation of education are now an ongoing feature across Scotland in response to the funding allocations for local government services. In Stirling, as with many other local authorities, this has led to a loss of early learning expertise at the most senior levels in the service. The impact is that the strategic leadership of early years provision comes from a more generalist, and therefore, 'schools' perspective and values base. This may result in a much greater emphasis on education outcomes and less emphasis on the ways in which we think about and work with children and families. This has also led to a reduction in the knowledge base at the strategic senior management level of the organisation as very few senior education managers understand or are knowledgeable about pedagogical documentation.

Changes to the wider corporate organisation and the reduction in the strategic leadership and management team, mean that again there is no one with the specialist knowledge and understanding of early years at this level in the organisation. This has also meant the loss of the connections and networking nationally and internationally. There is no doubt that in taking forward a model of pedagogical documentation this could be viewed as a significant loss. However, it forces us to consider other ways in which we can continue to sustain this approach. One way we can do this is to see this as Edgar Cahn says, as a 'change in characteristics and therefore a change in dynamic'. This means of course that we can also create a 'new dynamic'.

Malaguzzi, L. (2000) *The Hundred Languages of Children*, Reggio Children.

McLaren, P. and Leonard, P. (eds) (1993) *Paulo Freire: A Critical Encounter*, Routledge Falmer.

National Association for the Education of Young Children and Fred Rogers Center for Early Learning and Children's Media at Saint Vincent College (2011) 'Technology and interactive media as tools in early education programs serving children from birth through age 8', Position Statement.

Moss. P, and Petrie, P. (2002) *From Children's Services to Children's Spaces: Public Policy, Children and Childhood*, Routledge Falmer.

Plowman, L., Stevenson, O., Stephen, C. and McPake, J. (2011) 'Preschool children's learning with technology at home', *Computers & Education*, 59(1), 30–37.

Pope Edwards, C., Gandini, L. and Forman, G. (1998) *The Hundred Languages of Children: the Reggio Emilia Approach – Advanced Reflections*, 2nd Edition, Ablex.

Pound, L. (2005) *How Children Learn: From Montessori to Vygotsky – Educational Theories and Approaches Made Easy*, Step Forward Publishing.

Rinaldi, C. (2002) 'An audience with Carlina Rinaldi', MacRobert Arts Centre, Stirling University, September.

Rinaldi, C. (2006) *In Dialogue with Reggio Emilia, Listening, Researching and Learning*, Routledge.

Rinaldi, C. (2013) *Re-Imagining Childhood: The inspiration of Reggio Emilia Education Principles in South Australia*, South Australian Government. Available online at: www.thinkers.sa.gov.au/rinaldiflipbook/files/inc/d99b4762d1.pdf (last accessed 20 November, 2014).

Rogoff, B. (1990) *Apprenticeship in Thinking: Cognitive Development in Social Context*, Oxford University Press.

Scottish Government (2008) *Early Years Framework*, Scottish Government.

Stirling Council (2001) *Children as Partners*, Stirling Council Children's Services.

Stirling Council (2003) *Working with Documentation*, Stirling Council Children's Services.

Sully, A. (2006) 'Role and responsibility of documentation', *Re-Focus Journal* 3.

Trebeck, K. (2011) *Whose Economy? Winners and Losers in the New Scottish Economy*, Oxfam GB.

Thornton, L. and Brunton, P. (2009) *Understanding the Reggio Approach: Early Years Education in Practice*, 2nd Edition, Routledge.

United Nations Convention on the Rights of the Child (UNRC), Article 12.

UNICEF (2006) *Implementing Childs Rights in Early Childhood*, Bernard Van Leer Foundation.

Vecchi, V. (2010) *Art and creativity in Reggio Emilia: Exploring the Role and Potential of Ateliers in Early Childhood Education*, Routledge.

Wien, C. A. (2011) 'Learning to document in reggio-inspired education', *Early Childhood Research & Practice*, 13(2).

Whalley, P. (2001) *Involving Parents in their Children's Learning*, Paul Chapman.

Index